LOSING A BABY

SARAH EWING is the former editor of a national parenting magazine. Since October 2001, she has worked as a freelance health, travel and features journalist, writing for *The Times*, the *Guardian*, the *Evening Standard*, the *Herald* and women's magazines such as *Red*, *Glamour*, *Top Santé*, *Healthy* and *Natural Health*. Her main areas of focus are pregnancy, allergies, diabetes, cancer and complementary therapies. She was the second journalist ever to interview the former head of MI5, Dame Stella Rimington. She lives in north London.

Overcoming Common Problems Series

Selected titles
A full list of titles is available from Sheldon Press,
36 Causton Street, London SW1P 4ST, and on our website at
www.sheldonpress.co.uk

Assertiveness: Step by Step
Dr Windy Dryden and Daniel Constantinou

The Assertiveness Handbook
Mary Hartley

Body Language at Work
Mary Hartley

Breaking Free
Carolyn Ainscough and Kay Toon

The Candida Diet Book
Karen Brody

Cataract: What You Need to Know
Mark Watts

The Chronic Fatigue Healing Diet
Christine Craggs-Hinton

Cider Vinegar
Margaret Hills

Comfort for Depression
Janet Horwood

Confidence Works
Gladeana McMahon

Coping Successfully with Irritable Bowel
Rosemary Nicol

Coping Successfully with Pain
Neville Shone

Coping Successfully with Panic Attacks
Shirley Trickett

Coping Successfully with Prostate Cancer
Dr Tom Smith

Coping Successfully with RSI
Maggie Black and Penny Gray

Coping Successfully with Ulcerative Colitis
Peter Cartwright

Coping Successfully with Your Hiatus Hernia
Dr Tom Smith

Coping with Alopecia
Dr Nigel Hunt and Dr Sue McHale

Coping with Anxiety and Depression
Shirley Trickett

Coping with Blushing
Dr Robert Edelmann

Coping with Bowel Cancer
Dr Tom Smith

Coping with Brain Injury
Maggie Rich

Coping with Bronchitis and Emphysema
Dr Tom Smith

Coping with Candida
Shirley Trickett

Coping with Childhood Allergies
Jill Eckersley

Coping with Childhood Asthma
Jill Eckersley

Coping with Chronic Fatigue
Trudie Chalder

Coping with Coeliac Disease
Karen Brody

Coping with Cystitis
Caroline Clayton

Coping with Down's Syndrome
Fiona Marshall

Coping with Dyspraxia
Jill Eckersley

Coping with Eczema
Dr Robert Youngson

Coping with Endometriosis
Jo Mears

Coping with Epilepsy
Fiona Marshall and
Dr Pamela Crawford

Coping with Fibroids
Mary-Claire Mason

Coping with Gallstones
Dr Joan Gomez

Coping with Gout
Christine Craggs-Hinton

Coping with Incontinence
Dr Joan Gomez

Coping with Long-Term Illness
Barbara Baker

Coping with the Menopause
Janet Horwood

Overcoming Common Problems Series

Coping with a Mid-life Crisis
Derek Milne

Coping with Polycystic Ovary Syndrome
Christine Craggs-Hinton

Coping with Postnatal Depression
Sandra L. Wheatley

Coping with SAD
Fiona Marshall and Peter Cheevers

Coping with Snoring and Sleep Apnoea
Jill Eckersley

Coping with Strokes
Dr Tom Smith

Coping with Suicide
Maggie Helen

Coping with Teenagers
Sarah Lawson

Coping with Thyroid Problems
Dr Joan Gomez

Coping with Thrush
Caroline Clayton

Curing Arthritis – The Drug-Free Way
Margaret Hills

Curing Arthritis – More Ways to a Drug-Free Life
Margaret Hills

Curing Arthritis Diet Book
Margaret Hills

Curing Arthritis Exercise Book
Margaret Hills and Janet Horwood

Depression at Work
Vicky Maud

Depressive Illness
Dr Tim Cantopher

Eating for a Healthy Heart
Robert Povey, Jacqui Morrell and Rachel Povey

Effortless Exercise
Dr Caroline Shreeve

Fertility
Julie Reid

The Fibromyalgia Healing Diet
Christine Craggs-Hinton

Free Your Life from Fear
Jenny Hare

Getting a Good Night's Sleep
Fiona Johnston

Heal the Hurt: How to Forgive and Move On
Dr Ann Macaskill

Heart Attacks – Prevent and Survive
Dr Tom Smith

Help Your Child Get Fit Not Fat
Jan Hurst and Sue Hubberstey

Helping Children Cope with Attention Deficit Disorder
Dr Patricia Gilbert

Helping Children Cope with Change and Loss
Rosemary Wells

Helping Children Cope with Grief
Rosemary Wells

Helping Children Get the Most from School
Sarah Lawson

How to Accept Yourself
Dr Windy Dryden

How to Be Your Own Best Friend
Dr Paul Hauck

How to Cope with Bulimia
Dr Joan Gomez

How to Cope with Difficult People
Alan Houel and Christian Godefroy

How to Improve Your Confidence
Dr Kenneth Hambly

How to Keep Your Cholesterol in Check
Dr Robert Povey

How to Make Yourself Miserable
Dr Windy Dryden

How to Stand up for Yourself
Dr Paul Hauck

How to Stick to a Diet
Deborah Steinberg and Dr Windy Dryden

How to Stop Worrying
Dr Frank Tallis

How to Untangle Your Emotional Knots
Dr Windy Dryden and Jack Gordon

Hysterectomy
Suzie Hayman

The Irritable Bowel Diet Book
Rosemary Nicol

Is HRT Right for You?
Dr Anne MacGregor

Letting Go of Anxiety and Depression
Dr Windy Dryden

Lifting Depression the Balanced Way
Dr Lindsay Corrie

Overcoming Common Problems Series

Living with Alzheimer's
Tom Smith

Living with Asperger Syndrome
Joan Gomez

Living with Asthma
Dr Robert Youngson

Living with Autism
Fiona Marshall

Living with Crohn's Disease
Dr Joan Gomez

Living with Diabetes
Dr Joan Gomez

Living with Fibromyalgia
Christine Craggs-Hinton

Living with Food Intolerance
Alex Gazzola

Living with Grief
Dr Tony Lake

Living with Heart Disease
Victor Marks, Dr Monica Lewis and
Dr Gerald Lewis

Living with High Blood Pressure
Dr Tom Smith

Living with Hughes Syndrome
Triona Holden

Living with Nut Allergies
Karen Evennett

Living with Osteoarthritis
Dr Patricia Gilbert

Living with Osteoporosis
Dr Joan Gomez

Living with Rheumatoid Arthritis
Philippa Pigache

Living with Sjögren's Syndrome
Sue Dyson

Losing a Baby
Sarah Ewing

Losing a Child
Linda Hurcombe

Make Up or Break Up: Making the Most of Your Marriage
Mary Williams

Making Friends with Your Stepchildren
Rosemary Wells

Overcoming Anger
Dr Windy Dryden

Overcoming Anxiety
Dr Windy Dryden

Overcoming Back Pain
Dr Tom Smith

Overcoming Depression
Dr Windy Dryden and Sarah Opie

Overcoming Guilt
Dr Windy Dryden

Overcoming Impotence
Mary Williams

Overcoming Jealousy
Dr Windy Dryden

Overcoming Procrastination
Dr Windy Dryden

Overcoming Shame
Dr Windy Dryden

Overcoming Your Addictions
Dr Windy Dryden and
Dr Walter Matweychuk

The PMS Diet Book
Karen Evennett

Rheumatoid Arthritis
Mary-Claire Mason and Dr Elaine Smith

The Self-Esteem Journal
Alison Waines

Shift Your Thinking, Change Your Life
Mo Shapiro

Stress and Depression in Children and Teenagers
Vicky Maud

Stress at Work
Mary Hartley

Ten Steps to Positive Living
Dr Windy Dryden

Think Your Way to Happiness
Dr Windy Dryden and Jack Gordon

The Traveller's Good Health Guide
Ted Lankester

Understanding Obsessions and Compulsions
Dr Frank Tallis

When Someone You Love Has Depression
Barbara Baker

Work–Life Balance
Gordon and Ronni Lamont

Your Man's Health
Fiona Marshall

Overcoming Common Problems

Losing a Baby

Sarah Ewing

First published in Great Britain in 2005

Sheldon Press
36 Causton Street
London SW1P 4ST

Copyright © Sarah Ewing 2005

British Library Cataloguing-in-Publication Data

A catalogue record for this book is available from the British Library

ISBN 0–85969–928–5

1 3 5 7 9 10 8 6 4 2

Typeset by Deltatype Limited, Birkenhead, Merseyside
Printed in Great Britain by
Ashford Colour Press

Contents

Acknowledgements   ix

Introduction   xi

1 Understanding what happened   1

2 Saying goodbye   15

3 Taking care of yourself   22

4 Coping with the outside world   27

5 Fathers   37

6 Coping as a couple   48

7 Telling your other children   57

8 Complementary therapies for grief   63

9 Planning for another baby   75

Useful Addresses   94

Further Reading   111

Index   115

Acknowledgements

Many thanks to the following experts and organizations whose invaluable knowledge helped me write this book:

- Professor Anthony Joyce, University of Alberta, Canada;
- Professor James Walker, St James University Hospital, Leeds;
- Dr David Liu, City Hospital, Nottingham;
- Dr Jane Wilson, Kingston Hospital;
- The Foundation for the Study of Infant Deaths (FSID);
- The Child Bereavement Trust;
- Dr Susan Nolen-Hoeksema, University of Michigan, USA;
- The Miscarriage Association;
- Kathy O'Brien, bereavement counsellor;
- Dr Teri Schwartz, clinical psychologist, New York, USA;
- Phillip Hodson, the British Association for Counselling and Psychotherapy;
- Dr Cheryl Milford, Magee-Women's Hospital, Pittsburgh, Pennsylvania, USA;
- Dr Liz O'Donnell, clinical counsellor;
- Dr Paula Hall, Relate.

Most of all, thanks to my parents, Mhorag and Gordon, who have helped me through my grief.

Introduction

If grief is the price we pay for love, as the bereavement expert Colin Murray Parkes says, then many newly bereaved parents may feel that the price is just too high. Losing your baby means losing a part of yourself. It means losing your dreams – not just your own private dreams, but dreams involving your family life. Sometimes you may not even be fully aware of all those dreams until you know that the baby is irrevocably gone. Then the impact can be overwhelming. This slow living through all the implications of your loss is what makes up grief. Grief is indeed hard work. It has to be done on a daily basis; it is tiring, and it takes time. And there are so many strands to it – anger, questioning, blame, and the sheer shock of new life being blotted out.

Nobody prepares you for this possibility when you're pregnant. Pregnancy is meant to be a happy experience, in which you bloom because you've got another little person growing inside you. You're looking forward to starting a family. Many hopes are intertwined with this burgeoning new life.

But then all your hopes are taken away from you, leaving you desolate. Suddenly you're mourning the loss of your bright future and all the rites of passage you won't experience, from your baby's first bath to her first birthday party. Perhaps one of the most difficult aspects of this raw grief is that sometimes there may be no answer to 'Why?'

In time, as grief is lived through, it is possible eventually to accept that sometimes there are no reasons for your loss that you can put into words, that this may happen to anyone and does happen to many people, and that life is precious and not to be taken for granted. The main point to bear in mind for now is not to blame yourself. Many bereaved parents go through much anguish as they ask themselves whether anything they did or didn't do was to blame for the loss of their child, or, more subtly, whether their loss is due to some inherent defect in themselves – some past sin or crime, for which they are now undergoing punishment. Irrational though it may be when put like this, this sense of guilt is common, but misplaced.

Another point is isolation. Expressions of grief are so taboo in our society that sometimes it's hard to grieve properly. You may feel that no one understands and no one cares, especially when you encounter comments such as, 'It's not as if the baby was even a person yet.' But your baby was very real to you. He or she was a person with a developing personality. You had bonded with that baby, and had imagined what your future together would be like. Now, you may feel as if you belong to some secret club that no one wants to join. Yet, more than 250,000 couples go through this every year in the UK. You are not alone.

I hope that this book will help you come to terms with your loss. Too many books on this subject can end up sounding like impersonal medical textbooks. I wanted to humanize my book, to give grief a face and a name. You'll find the stories of many mothers and fathers (the latter are too often ignored) throughout the book to show you that you're not alone, and that there are many different ways of grieving and coping. I hope you may be able to think about these points and discuss them with your partner. But I also want to give you the latest information on miscarriage, stillbirth and cot death, to help you make a more informed decision about getting pregnant again.

Losing your baby might feel like the end of the world. After reading this book, I hope you'll feel that, while one world may end, other worlds do lie ahead. The baby who's gone – the special one who didn't make it – will always hold a unique place in your heart. But your heart can expand to make room for more life. Your decision to go on after losing your baby does indeed in time become a tribute to your love.

1

Understanding what happened

Losing your baby is one of the most devastating experiences you'll ever have to go through, and, very often, it's something for which you are totally unprepared. Instead of the happy ending you were looking forward to so much, you now have to contend with shock and disbelief. How could this happen to me? I did everything I was supposed to. Why didn't things go as planned?

Losing a baby makes you realize you're not in control of your life. We believe we can control our destiny if we try hard enough, but sometimes fate takes the control away from us, leaving us overwhelmed and confused. If you're looking for answers and searching to make some sense of your confusion, then this chapter will help you understand what's happened to your body and your baby.

Miscarriage: facts at a glance

- 20 per cent of all pregnancies end in miscarriage.
- 75 per cent of all miscarriages happen in the first trimester.
- 250,000 miscarriages occur every year in the UK.
- Recurrent miscarriages happen to just under 2 per cent of women.
- Miscarriage risk increases with age: 25–29, 10 per cent risk; 30–34, 12 per cent; 35–39, 18 per cent; 40–44, 34 per cent; 45+, 53 per cent.

Miscarriage: what happened?

In many cases, doctors can't give a definite cause for miscarriage. It's natural to search for cause and effect, and to ask yourself whether anything you did could have caused the miscarriage. Rest assured that this is very rarely the case. While sadly there may be no answer to your 'Why?', the vast majority of miscarriages do happen of their own accord – 'spontaneous' is the medical word for this, and does convey the idea that in many cases miscarriage 'just happens'. Most women who have a miscarriage go on to have a successful pregnancy next time.

Searching for answers can be extremely frustrating. Knowing why it happened can help your grief, and can also help you plan your next pregnancy with the aim of preventing a recurrence. Eventually, however, many women find they simply have to accept that they might never know. This can represent a turning point in grieving.

Miscarriage is defined as losing a baby up to around the 24th week of pregnancy, although thanks to modern medicine some babies born earlier than this date do survive. After 24 weeks the loss of a baby is considered a stillbirth.

Miscarriage is very common. At least one in four women who become pregnant will experience a miscarriage, and some doctors estimate that as many as 50 per cent of all pregnancies end in miscarriage, with many happening before the woman knows she is pregnant.

A look at early loss

Jodie
I had four miscarriages between the birth of my daughter and son. I wasn't having any trouble conceiving, just keeping my babies longer than eight weeks. Even though they were early losses, it was like losing a piece of me every time.

A cause was never found – a blood test after my fourth was inconclusive, so I assumed it was a chromosomal abnormality. One thing that always sticks in my mind is lying in the bath after I had a scan, which showed my baby still there, but bleeding profusely. I was just crying and crying and begging for my baby to be OK.

The second time I was still hopeful, but nervous, and I kept doing pregnancy tests to make sure I was still pregnant, even though I knew pregnancy hormone levels can take weeks to drop after a miscarriage. Seeing those two lines on the test was reassuring in a way. When I started to bleed I was so upset because I just couldn't believe it was happening again. The bleeding got heavier and redder, but I just couldn't face going back to my GP.

The third and fourth times, I was five weeks gone and had only known for a week that I was pregnant, but I was still hopeful. Underneath I was just waiting for something to happen.

It's hard to describe the worry and nervousness that was always with me. Every time I went to the loo, I was checking for blood, waiting to see it, and every time I felt something I thought it was blood.

I still wonder why it happened to me. I just can't understand. I did all the right things – no smoking, no drinking, took things easy and gave up certain foods, but it made no difference.

Early miscarriage – causes

Many women are left in Jodie's position – they did all the right things, but to no avail. Much of the time, as I've said, we just don't know why miscarriage happens. The main reasons we know about include:

Genetic problems

This is by far the most common cause of miscarriage, ending an estimated 95 per cent of pregnancies where the babies have a genetic abnormality – perhaps nature's way of ending a non-viable pregnancy. For example, around half of all chromosomal problems are trisomies – where there are three copies of one of the chromosomes instead of the usual two – and trisomy of chromosome 16, the most common, is incompatible with life. Hard though it is to accept, some pregnancies just cannot survive.

The vast majority of chromosomal problems happen by chance and are unlikely to recur, which means there is a very good chance that things will go right next time. There is an increased risk in older mothers, but this can be counterbalanced by taking care of yourself and leading a healthy lifestyle (see Chapter 9, 'Planning for another baby').

Rarely, chromosomal abnormalities are inherited, more likely in the case of repeated miscarriages or if there is a known genetic condition in the family. Genetic testing can help identify the problem, in which case genetic counselling can be offered.

Hormonal problems

Low levels of the hormone progesterone, the hormone that prepares the lining of the uterus to support the fertilized ovum, have been associated with early miscarriage. Progesterone treatment has been the standard treatment for this though some experts now disagree about its effectiveness.

Immune system problems

This is when your body perceives the fertilized ovum (half made up of foreign genetic material from the father) as an intruder, and accordingly rejects it.

Certain auto-immune diseases, such as lupus (systemic lupus erythematosus, SLE), also increase the risk of miscarriage. A blood test can tell whether certain antibodies are present that will make miscarriage more likely.

Blighted ovum

A blighted ovum occurs when a fertilized egg doesn't develop into an embryo or foetus, even although there is a placenta, so your pregnancy sac is empty. This happens because there aren't enough of certain proteins that are necessary for development.

Other causes

These are many and may simply not be known. Environmental stress is thought to be a factor by some, as it can affect the production of various brain chemicals, and thus pregnancy hormones. Problems stemming from the father are also thought to be implicated in some cases, with abnormalities in the sperm being a contributory factor in an early miscarriage.

Later miscarriage

The causes of a miscarriage in the second trimester are slightly different. They are usually due to problems with the uterus or cervix.

Structural problems

A small or mis-shaped uterus can usually be corrected with a simple operation, and the majority of pregnancies are successful after surgery. If your cervix isn't strong enough (incompetent cervix) your baby's growth puts pressure on it and it widens too early in pregnancy, breaking the waters and releasing the baby too soon. About 20 per cent of second trimester losses are due to cervix problems. Recurrence can be prevented by means of a reinforcing stitch in the cervix at the end of your first trimester, so you can carry to term.

Chromosome problems

These also cause approximately 20 per cent of second-trimester miscarriages.

Illness

This rarely causes miscarriage today but some undiagnosed and/or untreated conditions are linked to a higher risk of late miscarriage, such as high blood pressure, disease of the kidneys, diabetes and thyroid problems. Prolonged high fevers or infections in the mother may also affect a developing baby, such as rubella (German measles), herpes simplex and chlamydia.

Follow-up treatment

Depending on when and how your pregnancy ended, you may be offered a follow-up appointment at the hospital. Your doctor may recommend blood tests, though this is more likely in the case of later or recurrent miscarriage than early miscarriage.

If you're not offered any follow-up treatment, you may want to make an appointment with your GP, midwife or health visitor to discuss any worries or questions. Pre-pregnancy counselling may also be an option especially if you have known genetic factors in the family.

Kate

I already had two children, and was only nine weeks into my next pregnancy when I saw a small patch of watery brown blood when I went to the toilet. I started to panic, so my partner phoned for an emergency doctor, who came out to see me. He booked me in for a scan the next day, but strangely they said they could see my pregnancy sac, but that my baby was measuring only six weeks old. They couldn't detect a heartbeat, but they said to come back in a week for another scan.

A few days later, I had very bad pains all day, just like labour pains. Eventually, I felt an urge to go to the toilet and as I sat down, I miscarried. I went for an urgent scan the next day at the hospital and it showed that I'd had a complete miscarriage, which was lucky in a way, as I didn't need to have a D&C (dilation and curettage, or scraping the lining of the womb).

I kept thinking it was my fault and I started to think that I'd lost the baby as punishment for not planning my pregnancy. I had very little official support, apart from a hospital leaflet. I got the impression that miscarriage is just mundane to the doctors because they see it every day. When I was waiting for my first scan, I was in a waiting room full of pregnant women and when I came out, having been told there was no heartbeat, I found this very distressing. I've since found out some friends have also had miscarriages, so I can turn to them now.

Recurrent miscarriage

Sadly, you may have had more than one miscarriage. Statistically, this is quite rare – only 5 per cent of couples have two miscarriages and only 1 per cent have three or more – but if it happens to you, you'll know only too well the bleakness and anxiety that lie behind the cold numbers. The good news is that tremendous breakthroughs have been made in the last couple of years in discovering what causes women to have more than one miscarriage. As a result, a series of tests can reveal the underlying cause more than 75 per cent of the time, which can help put your mind at ease. Some doctors wait until you've had three or more miscarriages to order these tests, but you can ask for them to be done after two miscarriages.

There are four main causes for recurrent miscarriages: chromosomal problems (up to 60 per cent), problems with your uterus (10– 15 per cent), hormone problems (between 5 per cent and 40 per cent of early pregnancy loss) and immune system problems (5– 10 per cent), which have been explained above.

How long does it take to recover

The earlier in the pregnancy a miscarriage occurs, the more quickly your body will return to normal, although the devastating emotional effects will still be there. After the miscarriage, you may bleed and have pains for up to two weeks. If they become worse, if there is an unpleasant vaginal discharge or if you have a high temperature, contact your doctor as soon as possible, since these may be signs of an infection.

Pregnancy hormones normally take one to two menstrual cycles to work their way out of your bloodstream. You can expect to have your first period around six weeks after your miscarriage, and this may be heavier than usual.

One particularly upsetting factor after a later miscarriage or stillbirth is coping with lochia (blood loss) and heavy breasts which may leak milk for several days after your loss. A supportive bra, a warm bath and paracetamol can all help. If you are very uncomfortable or worried, ask your GP for advice.

Other early pregnancy losses

Ectopic pregnancy

Ectopic pregnancy is when the fertilized egg or embryo from your ovaries has implanted in one of your fallopian tubes on the way to your uterus. Around one in every 200 pregnancies is ectopic. This needs urgent medical attention. Common symptoms are abdominal pain, dizziness or fainting, and bleeding. Luckily, ectopic pregnancies are usually diagnosed early, and your doctor can prescribe a drug that can dissolve the embryonic tissue without harming your tubes and other internal organs. Surgery is necessary for those further along in pregnancy. Even though this situation is potentially life-threatening for the mother, it can be traumatic to accept the need for surgical intervention. Many women feel guilt at signing the consent forms even though it was the only possible action they could have taken.

Molar pregnancy

This is another cause of early pregnancy loss and is very rare. Normally, an egg divides equally into tissue for the placenta and the tissue that becomes your baby. However, in a molar pregnancy, there isn't an even split and there ends up being a very large placenta with only a small amount of tissue – or none at all – to start your baby off. What happens is that the placenta can then grow like a tumour, if you don't miscarry first. You will need surgery called a D&C (dilation and curettage), which is done under anaesthetic.

If you've had either an ectopic or a molar pregnancy, you may have problems conceiving again, although it doesn't mean you can't get pregnant again. It will take you longer to recover physically and some doctors recommend you wait between six months and a year before trying again.

Sarah

I've had two miscarriages and one ectopic pregnancy. With my first, I only had a tiny bit of spotting at eight weeks. Luckily, I was due for a scan. They said they couldn't hear a heartbeat, but there was a 50–50 chance that everything would be all right. Two and a half weeks later, when I went for another scan, they said my baby hadn't grown and there was definitely no heartbeat, so I had a D&C. I felt as if my world was caving in because I'd already planned everything for this baby.

With my ectopic pregnancy, my period was late so I did a pregnancy test, which was positive. My pain started the next day, so I went to an emergency doctor who sent me straight to the hospital. They did a pregnancy test, which now came up negative. I started bleeding the next day and a scan revealed the foetus in my ovary. My notes say a miscarried ectopic. I was astounded. We hadn't been trying for a baby so it was a surprise pregnancy. But within the space of a day I'd become really excited about this new baby. I didn't understand how this could be happening to me again. I began to wonder if there was something wrong with me.

With my final miscarriage, my husband and I had just started trying for a baby. I'd done several pregnancy tests just to be sure and they all came back positive. I went to my GP immediately, as I wanted an early scan because of my risk. He did a beta blood test a test to measure pregnancy hormones, which came back low. A week later I started the dreadful bleeding again; it was awful.

My GP was very good to offer to do the beta blood test, which isn't routinely offered. I did feel I was treated as an individual, which made me feel as if he actually cared. However, he seemed to run out of resources when the result came back low.

Stillbirth

In the UK, 16 babies a day are stillborn or die in the first four weeks of life, according to SANDS, the Stillbirth and Neonatal Death Society.

Women who see their baby on a scan, or who hold their stillborn child, may have to live with the haunting vision of a baby who looks

Stillbirth: facts at a glance

- In 2002, there were 3,727 stillbirths in the UK – a rate of 5.6 per 1,000 births.
- Women who give birth to low-weight babies are at increased risk of having a future stillbirth.
- Women who give birth by caesarean section for a non-medical reason increase their risk of a subsequent stillbirth.
- Drinking more than four cups of coffee a day while pregnant increases your risk of a stillbirth.

as if he is asleep, making it hard to take in that this peaceful, tiny figure is no longer living. So what went wrong? What could possibly have gone wrong? Stillbirth is much rarer today than in previous generations, and comes as an immense shock when it does happen. (This applies to medical staff as well as to mothers – World Health Organization (WHO) obstetric guidelines clearly recognize that this is a very disturbing event for all concerned including medical personnel, who are after all trained to preserve life. Unfortunately, as with other types of baby loss, some medical staff may not be adequately trained or supported themselves to deal with the event, and with their own reactions as well as yours – though others prove highly sensitive and supportive.)

While doctors are unable to find a reason for more than 50 per cent of stillbirths, there are three main reasons why a child may die:

Birth defects

These account for 10 per cent of stillbirths and usually involve the nervous system, brain and heart. Examples include water on the brain and anencephaly (a condition affecting the brain and skull bones that results in minimal development of the brain.) They can be due to chromosome problems or pre-existing genetic factors, of which you might have been unaware. Chromosome problems are largely chance events, and you have a 97 per cent chance of having a successful pregnancy next time. Tests will be done on both your and your partner's DNA to see if your genes are the cause. If they are, then you will get genetic counselling to help predict the risks involved in future pregnancies. If you have a family history of heart

9

problems, ask your doctor for a referral to a paediatric cardiologist for monitoring during your next pregnancy.

Problems with the placenta and umbilical cord

Your placenta is the vital channel for oxygen, water and nutrients from yourself to your baby. Sometimes the placenta can become dislodged, starving or suffocating your baby. Also, the umbilical cord can wrap itself round your baby's neck or develop a knot. These causes are fairly uncommon.

Pre-existing health problems with the mother

In the case of diabetes (not gestational or pregnancy-lined diabetes), high blood pressure or pre-eclampsia (a pregnancy disorder involving high blood pressure, see p. 42), poor circulation can limit blood oxygen supply to the baby. However, more research into these causes is needed.

Louise

My pregnancy was fine, apart from some minor bleeding at the beginning. My 20-week scan showed nothing wrong. I was very healthy and everything was progressing well, until 24 weeks and four days, when I bled. Eight days later, I gave birth to Louis. I had an emergency caesarean and he was born alive, weighing 1lb 2oz. Two days later he died.

I was told it was due to 'hyaline membrane disease', which is common in both premature babies and older people because basically the lungs can't cope. What I still don't know is why he was born so premature.

I was absolutely horrified. I burst into tears and felt completely helpless. I couldn't control what was happening. When he was born, I was so proud and I couldn't wait for visitors to come and see him. When he died, I saw no point in getting up each day.

It's been almost four years now and I don't think I'll ever stop grieving, but I just learn to cope with it. The first few months were awful. I was numb. I used to look out of my front window and see a world that was carrying on without me. People around me made me feel like a freak, and that Louis was 'just' a baby, so I shouldn't be grieving as much as if he had been older!

I still miss him, and think of him every day. I wonder what he'd be like now, and think how I'd love to see him playing in the garden with his little sister Lydia.

Finding out why your baby was stillborn

Investigating the cause of death is a highly sensitive issue, and it is a very personal decision whether or not to have a post-mortem done on your baby. Many women feel they prefer simply to leave their baby in peace.

However, several relatively non-invasive tests can be done, including blood, chromosome, placenta and umbilical cord tests. An appointment is usually made around four to six weeks after the tests to discuss the results and how they could affect future pregnancies.

Michelle

When I was nearly 26 weeks pregnant, I was admitted to hospital because I'd been bleeding and was very uncomfortable. Two days after I was admitted, my waters broke and I was rushed to the delivery suite where they tried to delay the birth. My daughter's lungs weren't developed enough for her to survive. I named her Molly. I kept thinking, 'Why me? What have I done to deserve this?' I thought I would wake to find it had been a bad dream.

When we went back to the hospital, the consultant said that nothing was found in the post-mortem and it was just one of those things. However, ten months later a midwife at the local fertility centre told us it was caused by placental abruption (when the placenta comes away from the uterine wall).

At first my husband Rob hid his feelings and was there for me and our other daughter, Alicia (his step-daughter), who was six at the time. It really hit him, though, at Christmas, when we should have been sharing Molly's first Christmas, as she had been due on the 20th.

I've since gone on to have two other boys. My advice is, don't bottle up your feelings. Try and find other parents who have gone through the same thing because talking with others who understand what you're going through really helps. One day that black cloud will lift and you will smile and feel happier again.

Andrea

I lost my daughter at 37 weeks when I went into labour. She was stillborn. I hadn't felt any movement for a couple of days, but I was told not to worry, as this was normal leading up to labour. I found out I should have been taken straight into emergency for a caesarean. We later had every test possible and nothing seemed to be wrong, but they thought I'd had some sort of infection.

My initial reaction was shock, I didn't cry. I was numb for a couple of days, then I felt extremely low. I stayed in bed and cried because I felt as if someone had taken my heart out. It took months for this intense feeling to fade. My husband just tried to stay strong for me, but he cried too, and we often cried together.

I wish I'd trusted my instinct when I thought something was wrong, but the loss has brought my husband and me closer together emotionally because we are more open. We communicated and never suppressed our feelings because it's better out than in.

Cot death: facts at a glance

- Seven babies die of cot death every week in the UK.
- It is the leading cause of death of babies under a year – more than road accidents, leukaemia and meningitis combined.
- 90 per cent occur under the age of six months.
- Boys are more at risk.
- January to March are peak months. Cot death is least likely to occur July to September.
- Smoking during pregnancy increases cot death risk by up to 15 times.

Cot death: what happened

According to the Foundation for the Study of Infant Deaths (FSID), cot death is the sudden and unexpected death of your baby for no obvious reason. This is every parent's nightmare – an apparently healthy and happy baby lost from one day to the next. A post-mortem can help narrow down the potential reasons, as mentioned above in the stillbirth section, but again it's not a precise science. Environmental factors are thought to be involved, such as parental smoking and the heat of the baby's bedroom. However, scientists have also linked cot death with genetic factors.

The official FSID guidelines on cot death are:

- Place your baby on her back.
- Don't smoke in the baby's room.
- Keep the baby's head uncovered.
- Place the baby with feet to the foot of the cot.
- Preferably let your baby sleep in a cot in your bedroom for the first six months, not in your bed.
- Don't let your baby get too hot – the correct room temperature should be between 16°C and 20°C.
- A well-fitting cotton or acrylic sleeping bag is better than a duvet.

Emma

My pregnancy was fine. I was so well all the way through. Eve was born on 4 November, following induction, as she was two weeks overdue and my blood pressure had risen slightly in the last few days.

The labour was fine and for the next four months everything was great. I returned to work as a nurse following my maternity leave and I was working a night shift that fateful night. At 8 p.m., I'd left my husband Andy and Eve playing and I wasn't due to return until 7.30 a.m. the following morning. Eve was her usual happy, hungry self and looked fine. Andy fed her before putting her down to bed and again, as normal, at 4 a.m. When he woke up at 6.30 a.m., Eve was dead.

He instantly knew something was wrong, even before he opened his eyes, almost as if he had dreamt it. He attempted to wake her up, but she was already dead. In his shock, he didn't attempt resuscitation or even ring an ambulance. He was in the house alone and rang me at work and said I had to return immediately. I was convinced he'd made a mistake. I drove home and rang for an ambulance on the way, which arrived before me. They didn't attempt resuscitation either.

My husband was guilt-ridden for a month afterwards because he thought he could have done something to prevent it from happening. My only thoughts were 'Why was I at work?' and 'Why did this have to happen when Andy was alone? Why couldn't we have dealt with it together?'

I find it better to talk constantly about Eve and what she was like – her unique personality that only those who knew her would understand. Andy finds even the mention of her name difficult. It's been an enormous strain on our marriage, and having no other children we have often felt our whole future has been taken away.

Andy was strong for me and I for him. We rarely cried together – one would always listen and be strong while the other broke down. I only hope that no one ever has to go through what Andy and I did. The best thing is to talk and be honest with each other with whatever you're thinking and feeling. You have to share it, otherwise you will go mad.

2

Saying goodbye

You may or may not meet your baby face to face. Depending at which stage your loss takes place, you may or may not have the opportunity to see, touch or hold him or her. But at no matter which stage it happens, you can say goodbye to your baby in a way that has dignity and meaning for you.

If your baby is stillborn or it becomes clear that he will not survive after birth, you may have decisions to make about the last hours you spend together. You may want to let him spend the rest of his time in your arms, perhaps skin-to-skin or at your breast. You may want other family members or friends to be with you in your baby's last moments, to take photos, perhaps to bathe or dress your baby.

Michelle
I wish I'd spent more time with Molly before she was taken away from me. As soon as she was born she was taken out of the room and I wasn't even told whether I'd had a boy or a girl until we made someone bring her back to us. I should have spent the night giving her all the love in the world that would have to last a lifetime.

In the shock of the event, many women miss this first and last meeting with their baby, and are maybe left just with fragmentary memories – the moment the baby was placed on their abdomen, perhaps a brief cuddle, fleeting impressions of soft skin and baby smell. Other women do not even have this – they are left only with the sensation of a pregnancy that ended before its time, and dreams of what might have been, with perhaps just a scan picture or two. At whatever stage it happened, many parents only fully realize the impact of what has happened weeks or months after the event. But it is never too late to say goodbye to your baby, and to honour his or her brief appearance in your life.

You can choose to say goodbye to your baby in whatever way you prefer – you can have a religious or non-religious service, in a church, at the graveside or even at home. Or you can have some other kind of event such as a day of quiet or planting a tree.

Legal requirements

If your baby died later in the pregnancy (after 24 weeks) or during or after birth, burial or cremation arrangements are necessary by law. This is an area where many parents feel just too dazed to cope. It may be the first time they have had to plan a funeral, or even the first time they have had to attend the funeral of a child. Often, in the first stages of shock and grief, they hand the whole affair over to the hospital authorities, and this can lift some of the burden at a time when parents feel totally overwhelmed. Sometimes this can be a source of regret later on. But it is never too late to hold such a ceremony – indeed, it may even be more helpful some time after the event, in helping you celebrate your baby's importance in your life, and release what has happened.

If you do hand arrangements over to the hospital, you may want to know what will happen to your baby. Many hospitals now follow guidelines such as those produced by SANDS or have their own guidelines and will treat your baby with respect. If at a later date you feel you need to know what happened to your baby, it may be worth contacting the hospital to ask; more hospitals now keep records of the arrangements made for exactly such a purpose.

Registering the death

If your baby was stillborn (i.e. born after 24 weeks), then the death must be registered within 42 days in England and Wales, and 21 days in Scotland. You will be given a Certificate of Registration of Stillbirth by the registrar. If you gave birth to a baby who died shortly after birth, both the birth and death must be registered within five days in England and Wales, and eight days in Scotland. Under extenuating circumstances, the registrar will extend this period.

Registration takes place at your local Registry of Births and Deaths. If you phone in advance, you can usually book an appointment, so you won't need to sit in the waiting room with other people. If your baby lived for a short while after birth, the hospital will have already given you something called a medical certificate of stillbirth or death. You need to bring this, along with their birth certificate (if applicable) and medical card.

You can get your partner or another family member to attend this appointment if you don't feel up to it. The registrar will then give you a certificate for burial or cremation, which the funeral director will need if you're planning a service.

Ceremony

A ceremony, such as a memorial service, funeral, baptism or other service, gives you an opportunity to say a special goodbye and accept the reality of what has happened. It also allows other family members and friends to share your sorrow.

You can have your baby christened or blessed while you are in hospital or you can have it done at the funeral. You will be given a baptism certificate.

For parents who want to remember their baby in a service without specific religious overtones, there is no legal requirement for a minister to be involved. Although by law you must have your baby buried or cremated, you are under no obligation to hold a funeral service, so if this is not for you don't let outside pressures force you into doing something that does not feel right for you and your baby.

If your baby was born before 24 weeks, it can be very distressing to feel that she has been denied any official existence at all, without even a birth or a death certificate to mark her brief life. But you can still have a funeral or some other form of service to mark her departure. It is entirely your choice, and you may need time to think about it. Don't feel pressured to make decisions quickly, and, if you need it, don't hesitate to ask a family member or close friend for help.

The type of service varies according to individual parents – apart from the requirement of burial or cremation after 24 weeks, there are no legal needs to comply with. So you might want a simple, informal graveside service, or perhaps a more elaborate ceremony, with a chance for family and friends to view the child, and to meet afterwards for a wake. Don't underestimate the importance of this kind of ritual in mourning – this means the personal ritual of people grieving together, or offering comfort and strength to the bereaved, not the ritual of costly equipment such as hearse, mourners' cars and coffins, though this can be important to some people. However, other parents feel too raw to mourn with others. Every well-meant comment hurts, and no one really seems to understand such an intimate grief. In this case, goodbyes are best kept private and within the immediate family.

In the case of a funeral, you might want to put items in your baby's casket such as photographs of your family, one of two identical stuffed animals (the other one being for you) or a letter or poem to your baby, expressing how much he or she was loved. What is important is that the ceremony or service – at the time or later – has meaning for you.

Miscarriage

If you had an early miscarriage, you may want to have a ceremony at a place that has special significance for you, such as your church, a garden or the place where you spent your honeymoon. Some parents prefer to have their own ceremony, perhaps planting a tree or performing some other symbolic act – Trudi and Ian, who lived by the sea, wrapped some memorabilia in a shawl (bootees, a lock of hair, a soft toy), placed a lighted candle on top, and sent it floating out into the waves. If you had a miscarriage, you can still have a more formal service for your baby if you wish, conducted by the minister of your choice. Some hospitals and churches have regular remembrance services for babies who have died, where you can have your baby's name read out, and perhaps light a candle. Your midwife, hospital chaplain or your own minister may be able to tell you more about this.

Other children

If you have other children, it can be a good idea to include them in planning the funeral because it will help them to grieve and make them feel included. They might want to do a reading or have a song played at the service, or include a favourite toy, poem or letter in your baby's casket. Explain to them what to expect at a funeral and how the day will progress, so that there are no surprises that might leave your children confused and upset.

Remembering your baby

Part of grief is not wanting to forget, and some people may even cling to grief as a last, bitter-sweet link with their baby. Many parents channel this need into some form of long-lasting memorial.

Depending on when your baby was born, you may or may not have been able to obtain mementos such as photographs, a lock of hair, or hand- or footprints. You may or may not have given your baby a name. While matters are handled more sensitively than in days gone by, too many women still feel they are rushed through the early days after baby loss – or they may be too dazed to think of anything but getting it all over with. They may be left only with a scan picture and a few toys that were meant for the baby; perhaps a choice of names.

But organizing such memories can be powerful medicine for your grief. There are many ways of remembering your baby, including treasured mementoes.

Michelle

I kept Molly's handprints and footprints, a hospital wristband and a little hat the same as the one she was buried in. I also got a necklace that splits into two halves – Molly was buried wearing one and her sister Alicia has the other. We've also got four photos of us together and we've kept a stillbirth certificate. I bought myself a necklace with a heart with footprints on it, and another with 'Mum' inscribed with an angel.

I mark Molly's memory when we send out cards to our family members, by putting a kiss from each of us and a bigger kiss from Molly. This is our symbol or silent word without upsetting anyone, as Molly is still a family member even though she is no longer in our lives to share.

Andrea

Every year we release a balloon on our little daughter's birthday. We have a photo of her in our room with an angel and a locket that contains her hair. I kept a few of her toys as well.

Emma

In hindsight, things happened too quickly. The police took Eve's sheets, bottles and food, even her yellow health visitor's baby book – which I signed to say I didn't wish them to be returned. Now of course I can't take that back and it's too late. But I've still got all of her other things and dozens of photographs. I love to hold her little cow with a rattle in it and I keep it by my bed. We put Eve's favourite toy, a stuffed octopus, in her casket, as well as photos of us all together.

Sarah

When I miscarried the first time, I kept a scrap book with my scan photos, a card I was given when I found out I was pregnant, my hospital bracelet and my pregnancy notes, but sadly I don't have any mementoes of the other two.

Donna

I kept a lock of Jowan's hair, a picture of him, his shawl and babygrow, as well as all the cards and letters I was sent, and the details of his funeral.

Some people remember their baby with a tree or a selection of plants at the grave; others may donate to a charity, especially one connected with the loss of a baby. Your hospital may have a book of remembrance, or you might like to make your own book of remembrance, with photos, poems and other writings from family and friends, and your own memories. Some women create their own memorial such as a garden, a quilt or a painting.

The Miscarriage Association has a tree of remembrance during Christmas, and also refers web page visitors to International Star Registry, via which it is possible to name a star in memory of your child (see Useful Addresses, p. 98). One couple went on a 'pilgrimage' to Germany, where their child had been conceived and where they had lived in their early married life, visiting places that had meaning and memories for them. It was painful, re-living former hopes and plans, but Susan and Robert felt they had honoured their child and their life together, and felt stronger when they returned.

Anniversaries and Christmas

An anniversary can happen at any time – six weeks, three months, six months, or just when it hits you. You do not have to wait for any specific time to remember your baby in a more formal or structured way.

Anniversaries may also take different forms – Una, who had two miscarriages, remembered the anniversary of each loss and each due date, and would read over poems she had written for her unborn children.

Some dates may be harder than others:

Donna
I find Mother's Day and Christmas harder than the anniversary of Jowan's death. I always go to church at Easter because that's around the time he died, and I take him flowers and plants for Christmas and Mother's Day.

Claire
The first anniversary was the hardest so far. It first hit me that it was real at six months and I had to have counselling, as I was naive about what to give my son and what to do for him. My

counsellor always gave me the advice, 'Do what you want to do, not what others expect you to do.'

At Christmas, we decided to visit his grave in the morning and take his presents that Santa had left and let the girls open them. We had a good cry, but then we realized we had to sort ourselves out for the girls, as it wasn't fair to be sad all day because it was still their Christmas too. We left our memories at the grave. We all jointly chose a gift for his first birthday, and had the number 1 done in beautiful lemon and white flowers. We let the girls release some balloons with a note attached to them, and sent them to Adam in heaven, because we said that is where God collects all the stray balloons and gives them to babies and children to enjoy.

But it isn't just anniversaries, important though they are – Adam forms part of our daily life. Adam's picture is on the wall between pictures of the girls, so people will see him straight away. He is very much part of our family, and friends and family know this. Friends especially will bring him into the conversation now and again. He is part of me and of our family and that's the way we talk about him.

3
Taking care of yourself

We grieve in the body as well as the mind, and the shock of what happened may leave you feeling chilled, scared and desolate to the core, especially after the physical and emotional upheaval of a pregnancy.

You may feel mistrustful of your body, or that it has let you down. Other physical symptoms of grief can include dizziness, insomnia, loss of appetite, palpitations, breathlessness, lack of concentration and fatigue. So you need to look after yourself both physically and emotionally. This said, you may find that you feel better physically before you recover emotionally. While the physical aspects of losing a baby are important, the emotional responses may be more profound and longer lasting as you mourn the destruction of real hopes and dreams for the future, and grieve not only for the baby who died but also for the life you may have imagined with the child.

It is well known that the new mother needs mothering – so does the woman who has just lost her immediate prospects of mother-hood. Now is the time for a great deal of comfort and comforting. Some of this will be available from others, but an important part of it you can give yourself.

Taking care of your body

The right physical care will help to restore your emotional balance. Do give yourself time to get back to normal – it can be very distressing to live through the real physical effects after a pregnancy has ended, including lochia, or blood flow, and milk coming into the breasts. Bear in mind that grieving can be hard work, and very tiring. It is important to get plenty of rest, even if you are reluctant to do so because you feel you ought to be getting on with life, or because you would rather not have quiet time in which to think. Do contact your doctor if you are concerned about your health.

Try to eat a balanced diet even if you don't feel that hungry, avoid junk food, and drink plenty of fluid, such as water or juice. Try to stay away from caffeine and alcohol which can cause dehydration and headaches – alcohol also slows your body and mind down, as well as dulling your natural emotions.

22

Exercise is important in creating and maintaining the energy you need to deal with your grief, and in releasing some of the associated tensions. Regular exercise can also help combat any feelings of loss of control which can be a feature of grief, so it may help to think in terms of, say, a morning walk or an afternoon swim. Aim to do one activity a day – a bike ride, stretching or a walk. Even gentle exercise is known to relieve depression. If you really want to release some pent-up anger, smashing glass at the bottle recycling or punching a beanbag at your gym are good ideas.

Your feelings: grief and depression

Experts sometimes speak of grief as a process with 'stages', patterns, timescales and outcomes. But there is no right or wrong way to grieve, and each person and family will have a unique way of expressing and coming to terms with their feelings. These feelings may include shock, despair, helplessness, sadness, loneliness, anger, disorientation, difficulty concentrating and panic.

Bear in mind that the very high levels of pregnancy hormones drop abruptly just after pregnancy loss, and this may contribute to your feelings. Progesterone and oestrogen, secreted by the ovaries and placenta, allowing the uterus to receive and maintain a fertilized egg, increase tenfold during pregnancy. After a pregnancy ends, progesterone levels drop dramatically, reaching pre-pregnant levels about 72 hours later. Such a major shift in hormones may well leave you very tearful and depressed for a few days. If you continue to feel very down, do consult your doctor, who can help you distinguish between depression and the course of grief. Other symptoms of depression include irritability, feeling you can't cope, sleeping difficulties and changes in appetite.

Donna
It wasn't a planned pregnancy and I was rather ambivalent about it to start with, but I just got on with it and enjoyed myself. My health was fine throughout, although I was rather scared there was something wrong.

Nine days after his due date, my lovely baby son Jowan was born. Four days later he was dead, from hypoplastic left heart syndrome. It's a congenital defect as a result of a chromosomal dysfunction. One in 3,000 babies is born with hypoplasia.

I was in shock; I just wanted to run away from it all. Secretly, I think my partner was relieved, although he didn't explicitly say so. He hadn't been too keen on the pregnancy to start with, and as he knew the seriousness of the diagnosis, the baby's death seemed to him to be the kindest ending to what happened, rather than him lingering on.

I didn't see it like that. I was furious and utterly miserable. I was incredibly angry with anyone who had children, who was pregnant, or even people who were married. I cried continuously for 48 hours.

I felt as if my arms had become alien. I didn't know what to do with them. I felt physically empty. It was as if I was inside a bubble and the rest of the world was completely beyond my comprehension. I wanted to be able to wear black armbands and to be public about mourning – but I couldn't. I just wanted the world to stop and to acknowledge this awful thing that had happened.

If you're grieving, get help. Professionals are paid to listen and they do it properly, allowing you to explore the issues that are really bothering you. Don't try and be stoical for your partner and don't ever deny the baby. He or she exists, even after death, and you are their parent, so they have the right to respect and recognition.

You can't run away from your grief. It's better to turn and face it in all the misery and pain, and find a way of living through it.

Not many people go through the whole of their lives being loved and cared for and doing nothing but bring joy. Your baby did. I would be proud to have such an epitaph.

Coping with your feelings

There may be work to be done in forgiving yourself and others for what has happened. Some women feel guilt for things they did or didn't do during the pregnancy, or go through remorse for any ambivalence they may have felt at being pregnant. Anger at doctors, justified or not, is another reaction. Other women may feel unable to see other mothers and babies, or go through feelings of sadness or anger when they do. Still others may feel even more guilty for times when they may feel happy, so 'betraying' their grief.

It may help to find out as much as you can about what happened to you, so do talk to your doctor and midwife, always remembering that only limited information may be available. If you do feel guilty, try and bear in mind that the loss is not your fault, or your body's fault, or the fault of your partner or your doctor. It is most unlikely that there is something you should have done differently. Genetic or medical complications are not a matter for blame and guilt. Viewing it in perspective, the pregnancy and birth processes are so complex, from the meeting of two cells to the formation of a new human being, that it is well-nigh miraculous that most of the time everything goes perfectly.

- Do find someone to talk to about your baby and your feelings – your partner, family and friends. Support groups such as the Miscarriage Association can be invaluable. Don't be afraid to ask for help. Family and friends may be pleased to know specific ways they can help, such as sharing childcare, shopping or just spending time with you. Let them share your grief.
- Reading books and articles can help with understanding, and help you feel less alone.
- Writing can be a good outlet for your emotions. You might want to start a diary of your thoughts and memories, or write letters or poems to your baby.
- Some couples are advised to get rid of all their maternity clothes and baby's belongings at once, but don't feel you have to do this until you are ready. Then, you might want to do this by means of a special ceremony which is your way of saying goodbye to your baby (see Chapter 2, 'Saying goodbye').
- If you are of a religious faith, this can be a daunting time. Some people feel that their religion or church has failed them. But this is the very time when your minister – or another – may be able to give support or help in renewing your faith, and in finding ways your faith can help you come to terms with your baby's death. Again, look at the suggestions for ceremonies in Chapter 2.
- It may be best not to make big decisions or changes during this time, and letting a few months to a year go by before making a major change is advisable.
- Don't let well-meaning others make your decisions for you, for example coming round to 'go through' the baby's things with you and bundle them all off to a charity shop. You and your partner are the only ones who know what you really want and need.
- Seek counselling, if you feel you need it, through your family

doctor, your hospital's bereavement counsellor or chaplain, or a therapist who specializes in grief and loss.

- Respect your needs and limitations as you work through your grief and begin to heal. Be aware that certain triggers can renew grief, such as meeting friends with babies, overhearing birth experience stories, doctor's visits, thoughtless comments, holidays and family reunions. Protect yourself by avoiding situations that you know will be difficult. You do not have to visit an old friend who has just had a baby if you don't want to.
- Remember, healing doesn't mean forgetting. Grief can be honoured in the healing process.

You have just been through a very painful experience. Allow yourself as much time as you need in which to recover both emotionally and physically, without forcing yourself to put on a brave face.

4

Coping with the outside world

At a time like this, the people you need around you are those who recognize what a tragic loss you've just had and will genuinely try to understand what you're going through, rather than giving you annoying or insensitive platitudes.

Unfortunately, in a crisis you often find out who your true friends are. Some might not know what to say and others will just not understand, especially if they feel you can simply 'try again'.

Many people don't understand that the baby was a person
This is a key factor behind many comments.

Sarah

I found people's reactions really upsetting, as I kept hearing 'It was really a baby at that stage, was it?' and 'Oh, no problem to try again.' I get really upset because it's so hard when people make such stupid, thoughtless comments. I don't force information about what has happened on to people, but if my experience can help I try and use it that way. I feel that way something good, if only small, has come out of it.

Michelle

I've become very thick-skinned to people's stupid remarks. But when Mitchell was born, my sister said, 'Oh how lovely, you and Rob are parents at last! How does it feel?' My reply was, 'He's our second child together because we are already Molly's parents.' And she said, 'Well, you know what I mean!' I told her that even though we had Mitchell now, this didn't change my love for Molly, and she just changed the subject.

Insensitive comments
Comments from others are a minefield in grief – sometimes those 'supportive' remarks are so fantastically unhelpful that you may be unsure whether to cry or to laugh. Classic insensitive comments include:

- 'It was God's will.'
- 'I'm sure it was for the best/a blessing in disguise.'
- 'You can always have another one.'
- 'Have you thought of getting pregnant again soon?'
- 'At least you weren't further along.'
- 'At least you'll see your baby in heaven some day.'
- 'You wouldn't have wanted the baby to be born deformed.'
- 'At least it wasn't a real baby.'
- 'It was better to lose it now, than later.'
- 'It wasn't meant to be.'
- 'Be thankful you already have a healthy child.'
- 'Why did you bother naming him?'

Some people may even question why you're having a funeral, baptism or memorial service because, in their words, 'It's not as if they were really a baby.'

Few bereaved parents want to hear this kind of 'consolation' from others. Unfortunately, there are many people who cannot bear to simply keep silent and just allow parents to grieve, without rushing in with these kinds of explanations and remarks. Such comments reveal how little people understand the grief of bereaved parents. One sad result is that you may find it hard or impossible to talk about what has happened, and this, of course, adds to your sense of aloneness and isolation.

Sarah
I found the hospital staff insensitive because they repeatedly said I was young and could try again.

Donna
I've become very blunt about talking about my loss with other people. They're often embarrassed and you find yourself having to put them at ease. I can't stand using euphemisms, like 'passed away'. My baby died. I am bereaved. That's it.

To begin with, people made stupid comments but they don't now because I challenged them. They'd say he was having his life elsewhere. This made me furious because I wanted to share his life with him. I was also told that I'd let myself go – and this was only two weeks after he died. I haven't been able to talk to that person again. I didn't want to be patronized. I knew I was angry; I didn't need to be given permission. This sounds as if I was really aggressive, but I wasn't. I was far too sad to be aggressive, but I couldn't let people get away with making these remarks. When I had my second son, some people said it didn't matter any more. I asked them how long a life has to be before it becomes important enough to matter.

If people aren't helping you, politely tell them that you would like to be on your own. Go with what you feel like and not what is expected of you. This might even include people like your parents.

Jodie

I had friends and family who said they were sorry and that they were there if I needed them, but I mainly coped alone. Some of my husband's family were very insensitive to my feelings. My sister-in-law even called us one Christmas Eve, a few days after one of my miscarriages, to tell us that she was pregnant. I still feel bitter about this.

You don't need these insensitive friends for now. It should quickly become apparent who they are, and sometimes it's the people you least expect who prove to be your best support.

Sue

When I was grieving I thought I was going mad at times. Unless you've experienced this intense pain yourself, you feel no one understands. Unfortunately, a couple of friends kept their distance from me. I suppose they didn't know what to say to me. I learned not to say anything to this kind of person. However, I found it very easy to talk to some people, and sometimes these were people I wouldn't really have considered as close friends before, such as the receptionist at work, who was an older lady with grown-up children. My perceptions of some people changed and I found new qualities to value in people. The one I liked best was the ability just to sit and quietly listen – no clever comments, no trying to put things right, no fidgeting with their watches. I really appreciated the people who would just give me time.

Even your nearest and dearest

Sometimes, in raw grief, those close to you just can't help putting their foot in it, and even loving comments can be misinterpreted as insensitive. This applies particularly to parents, who always want the best for their children, but who can't always travel along the same road of grief:

Rachel
I've had two miscarriages, and three terminations of our baby girls due to severe genetic abnormalities. The three babies had a genetic condition, called Jeune syndrome, a lethal form of dwarfism where the long bones are very short and the ribs are short and deformed, therefore stopping lung development. The prognosis given to me in all three cases was stillbirth or death immediately after birth from suffocation.

I still wish I hadn't shared my raw feelings with my family because I feel they all belittled my grief. After my first termination at 21 weeks, my dad told me I should be grateful because he knew someone who'd lost their son in a motorbike crash and that was worse. He also said that it wasn't as if my daughter was a proper baby. My mum just told me not to let it take over my life. She later admitted that they thought I should be grateful to get rid of an abnormal unborn baby. Even now I have feelings of anger towards them and it has affected the way I feel about them because I keep my emotional distance.

Even when adult, we can still be tempted to blame our parents for events that go wrong in our lives. However, while their loss may not be as intense as yours, grandparents do also grieve for the baby they will now never see, and you may need to allow for this in your contact with your family. Again, some form of ceremony can be useful in giving grandparents and close others a chance to grieve with you, but you may also want to find opportunities for talk later on in grief, when emotions may be slightly calmer and the temptation to hand out blame not so strong.

As time goes by

One problem that some mothers face is the assumption that, a few weeks or months after their loss, they must have recovered from the event and therefore no longer need support. People who may initially have been sympathetic no longer wish to talk about your baby, or may even appear to have forgotten all about it. Certain friends who may be very good to begin with can then become frustrated if you don't appear to 'get over' your loss. This can apply to your nearest and dearest – that is, your partner – as well as to more distant friends.

It can be particularly hard if your grieving 'timetable' has been 'out of sync' with others' attention and sympathy – for example, you may not have been able to talk at first just when others were overflowing with concern. Now that you feel ready, nobody wants to know.

Linda

Six months after Linda lost her baby boy at 25 weeks, it was business as usual. Her husband had ploughed back into work, she was back at her own job as a teacher, and none of her colleagues, friends or family so much as seemed to remember the event. Yet Linda felt that only now was she really feeling the full impact of her grief. She needed to talk!

There are different ways of handling this. In some cases, it may be that, below the surface, your partner actually needs to talk as much as you do, and would welcome a break from the silence. If you never found a way of saying goodbye to your baby, this might be something to consider together (see Chapter 2).

If your partner doesn't want to talk, you might take the decision to talk to a good friend, to discuss those shattered hopes and dreams, and to air any feelings of guilt or anger that may be hanging on.

In some cases, the best person to talk to is someone who's been through the same kind of loss, via a support group such as SANDS or the Miscarriage Association (see Useful Addresses). This is especially so if you do feel it is a little late in the day to talk to friends who appear busy with their own lives, or if you're just not getting the support you need from your usual contacts.

Bereavement counselling is another option, via your GP, hospital or a support group.

Bear in mind that this need to talk may continue at intervals long after the baby has gone. Grief has its own timetable and it is never too late to grieve.

Louise

People think I'm 'cured' because it's been four years since I lost my baby boy Louis at two days, and I've got a little girl now. Sometimes I'll be told, 'You've got over it well,' and I'll explain that I've haven't 'got over it' – I've just learnt to cope with the loss.

You will recover – but in your own time, so don't let anybody else's expectations of how long (or how short) you should be taking to grieve make you feel pressured. Life after such a loss will always be different to how it was before, and it takes time to adjust to this, too.

Getting the help you need from friends and family

It can help if, from the start, you are able to tell close friends and family clearly and simply how this has affected you, and that you'll need all their love and support in the coming months. It is important to state your needs and set your boundaries, even if it doesn't always stop the insensitive remarks or provide the support you need.

It's great to have one of those friendships where the other person knows how you're feeling without you having to spell it out. Unfortunately it's more likely that you'll have to tell your friends and family exactly what you need, whether it's some quiet time, or help with the chores and your other kids, or someone just to sit and keep you company.

Louise
At first I was worried that I'd embarrass people and they wouldn't know what to say, if it came up in conversation. Now I don't worry because I tell them the truth, and if they're embarrassed or apologize I just say it's not their fault, they weren't to know. I never hide it; it's usually one of the first things people find out about me. I find it hard to share my feelings, though, and it's very rare that anyone sees me upset.

Kate
Let people know that you want to talk about your loss and then they will feel more comfortable. Otherwise, they won't know what you want. You planned your baby's whole life so it's not just your baby you're grieving for, it's everything you've planned. It's all right to be upset.

Explaining may take more energy than you feel you have, but do try and share your feelings if you can. If you don't feel ready, don't worry. You are not obliged to if you feel too raw.

Try not to jump to conclusions about others' actions or inactions. People sometimes keep silent for the best of intentions. Most of your friends probably genuinely want to help you, but aren't sure how to best go about it, or might be afraid of saying the wrong thing, and so may say or do nothing. Your friends and family may think that not talking about the baby will take your mind off your loss, but we all know that this will have exactly the opposite effect. It's a really hard balance for others to strike, knowing when to say something and when to keep quiet.

If someone has unintentionally said something that has upset you, it may be best to air it immediately, so it doesn't fester. Allow yourself a couple of quiet minutes or go to the bathroom, and when you come back tell them as calmly as you can that they've said something you didn't think was right, and let them know how their statement made you feel. You may feel embarrassed or reluctant, but this is a time when it may be better for your emotional health to state your reactions openly.

Pregnant friends

Being unable to deal with your friends' pregnancies doesn't mean you have a jealous nature. It is possible, and natural, to feel happy for a friend who is having a baby, but sad for yourself. For the time being, though, it may help to avoid places where you know you'll run into lots of pregnant women or babies. Inevitably, you will see some, but until you feel less raw don't overdo things.

It can be especially difficult if any of your close friends are pregnant or are trying to get pregnant. Honesty may be the best policy here. Explain to your friend that you find her pregnancy hard to cope with in the light of your own experience. This may not be easy to confess, but your friend will appreciate your honesty much more than your silent avoidance.

Returning to work

Going back to work can signal a reassuring return to a structured environment where you are known and accepted, and where you have a certain, clear role to play. Work can sometimes provide a rest from grieving, especially if you have supportive colleagues. The first few days may, however, need some preparation. You may have to meet the questions of those who last saw you when you were pregnant, and to decide how much or how little explanation you want to give. Constant explanations can be draining. You may find it helpful to talk in advance with your closest colleagues, your boss or your personnel officer, and to provide a short, simple explanation of what happened with a view to pre-empting too much discussion when you do return. If you feel this is too much, or people do press you, just say that you're not ready to talk about it yet. Another possibility to consider is that of going back in stages, such as starting with half days or doing part-time if possible. Again, this is something to discuss before you go back.

You may also want to take in a few items that have meaning for you, such as a small photo of your baby; as well as having such significance for you, they can act as a signal to others of the reality of your loss, and perhaps deter some of the more insensitive comments you may encounter – or conversely, break awkward silences about what happened. If you don't want to make your loss this public, you might find it helpful to take in some private mementoes, such as a locket containing some of your baby's hair. Another idea is a small private journal in which to note down feelings of anguish or anger which it would be inappropriate to voice at work, or a book of poems or other reading you have found consoling.

Finally, you may well find that you return with a different view on life and may encounter others at work who have been through the loss of a baby. If so, you may be able to relate to them in a new way, and even offer them some of the comfort you need so badly yourself. By reaching out to them – when you are able – you may find you ease the pain of your own grief.

Getting other help

Sometimes, friends and family just can't give you the understanding and compassion you need, no matter how much they try. A parent support group or online message board will give you the opportunity to unburden yourself whenever you like, without constantly having to justify yourself or wondering if you're inconveniencing the other person by talking about something that can't be changed.

These groups can be your lifeline, reassuring you that you're not going crazy, that what you're feeling is normal, and that you're not over-reacting.

A 'live' parents' group with regular meetings will force you to get out of the house and not hide yourself away from the outside world. It's a step forward on your path to recovery. Ask your midwife or GP for a local group, or type 'miscarriage', 'stillbirth' or 'cot death support' into a search engine on the web. (See Useful Addresses.)

It can help if both you and your partner attend meetings. You might feel awkward at first, expressing raw emotions to complete strangers, but you're not trying to prove anything to these people – they are an unbiased sounding board for you.

You should also consider some one-to-one counselling because this will give you more time to air your feelings and work through personal issues, such as how you're coping as a couple. Don't think that you're a failure for turning to professional help in dealing with your loss. It is a brave step to admit that you can't cope – it's easier to put on a façade and say you're fine.

If you feel you are really losing control and are slipping into a deep depression, get help! Losing a baby is a heartbreaking experience, and you don't need to suffer alone. Speaking to a trained counsellor can help you work through your anger and guilt and help you get back on your feet again.

Jodie
I called the SANDS support line a couple of times the first year and they were great because they make you realize that you're not going mad, and it's confidential.

Get support from other people who have had similar losses and try to talk about it with people. Crying helps a lot, and reading poems that other women have written really touched me and made me feel as though someone else really understood.

How many children do you have?

Emma
At work I will undoubtedly have to face the question of 'Do you have children?' from strangers. I think I'll just reply 'No', because although it makes me shudder to deny Eve's existence, I feel it will be the only way to cope.

Louise

I've been asked several times if Lydia is my first or only child, and only once did I answer 'Yes'. I felt so guilty afterwards, as if I'd denied Louis' existence. I vowed never to do it again, and I haven't. I say, 'I had a son the year before Lydia, but he died when he was two days old.'

It may take thought to find a way of answering this question that has meaning for you, but, in the early stages, don't open the way to explanations you're not ready to give. The last thing you want is to have to repeat your story to people you don't know too well, especially if they don't know how to react, or react inappropriately.

Linda

In my experience I prefer to keep my dignity to begin with – you can always decide to tell more later if you choose. I find it best not to give too much away at first. I'll talk about my two living children and then, if the other person seems genuinely interested, or I feel I want to know him or her better, I may talk about the little son Stephan I lost at 25 weeks.

Sarah

If people ask, I say I have two children. However, depending on the situation and the people I am talking to, I may tell them I have also lost three babies.

Kate

I'm usually very open about my losses, except with pregnant women. I've had the typical comments from people that the twins would have been hard work and that I can always have more. The only thing people can and should say is, 'There is nothing I can say to make you feel better. I'm so sorry.'

Sarah

Some people are also uncertain as to whether they should call themselves 'parents' or not, though most people in this situation would agree that they undoubtedly are.

Your baby may have died, but the impact on your heart and your life remains. Parents do not forget. My advice for other parents is to talk about your baby and remember that you're still parents even if you don't have your baby with you.

5

Fathers

Just as fathers used to be excluded from the delivery rooms when their babies were being born, so they can feel very out of place when a baby dies. Much of the attention focuses on the mother, especially if there has been a medical problem, and more sympathy may be expressed for the mother. Concepts of grief mean that mothers are often expected to fulfil the grieving role, while fathers may be expected to be more stoical and take care of the practicalities of life such as telephoning family, friends and officials, registering the birth and death, and organizing any funeral and other arrangements.

However, when a baby dies, fathers often have a great deal to cope with. Not only are they grieving for their baby, they are also trying to help a partner who has just been through a vast emotional and physical upheaval. For many men, it can be very hard to get the balance right between supporting their partner and dealing with their own pain and grief. However, it is increasingly recognized how much men too need support and help while dealing with their own grief.

Two traps into which men may fall are:

- *Being strong for their partner*: many men feel they have to be the strong ones because this is what society expects. They may feel under pressure to hide their own grief as they support their partner, or may find themselves dealing with enquiries as to how the mother is rather than how they themselves are feeling. They may feel that they have no time or space to grieve – or permission.
- *Keeping busy*: someone has to make sure the day-to-day tasks are still done; or men may throw themselves back into their work or other activities.

Both routes can sometimes be a way for men to avoid dealing with their feelings and working through grief. But the grief and pain of fathers needs to be acknowledged too, both for their own sake and for the sake of their relationship as a couple (see Chapter 6, 'Coping as a couple').

This chapter is written specifically for fathers – so if men look at no other part of this book, this is the one chapter they should read!

Fathers could also benefit from reading the next chapter, too, even if they do not read the whole book. And this chapter is also good for women to read, as it does give an idea of how men may react – something which, as we've explored, can sometimes be overlooked.

For fathers

When you lose a baby, the attention is focused on your partner, and it may be hard to have your pain and grief acknowledged too. You are not less of a man for expressing your grief. It shows a level of self-assurance that you don't care about how society expects you to behave. Your pain will well up at unexpected times, but do give yourself permission to grieve. Sadly, many employers aren't as open-minded as they should be about fathers taking time off after the death of their baby, but don't feel bullied into going back sooner than you feel ready. Your health and that of your partner is more important.

It's normal to feel completely powerless in a situation like this, because the fate of your baby was taken completely out of your hands. To see your partner so hurt is also very difficult because you may feel you can't take away her pain. It's difficult to get the balance right between being there for her and having your pain and grief recognized too.

You might not have had the same emotional bond with your growing baby as did your partner, but you still had hopes and dreams for his or her future, and those have been crushed. Whatever you do, don't stop talking to your partner. Let her know how much you already loved your baby; it won't cause her any more pain. Expressing your grief to her shows you do care, and as long as you don't start channelling your anger at each other, then this can make you stronger. In fact, the emotional rawness and vulnerability can generate a level of closeness that would be otherwise hard to obtain. Do something every day for her, no matter how hard, that brings you closer together, even if it's just leaving her a Post-it note saying, 'I love you and we can get through this together.'

People's unfeeling comments can be distressing and infuriating, but try not to react. It might help to practise a phrase that you will repeat, calmly, every time this happens, such as 'I don't think that comment was very helpful,' and leave it at that. They should take the hint. If not, you could add, 'This is a very difficult time for us and it would really help if you would be more careful about what you say.'

If you're feeling angry, let it out by doing a vigorous sporting activity, hitting loads of golf balls or kicking a football, or going for a long walk somewhere quiet so you can clear your head or even shout if you want to.

Ask your GP if they know of any group therapy in your area, because knowing that there are other men out there who are going through or have been through the same thing can be a real comfort and help release your pent-up frustrations. You might find it hard opening up to strangers at first, but contrary to what you think, it can often be easier in a situation like this: you don't feel you have to hold back or that they have any preconceived notions about you. If you feel more at ease on the Internet, then there is one excellent international support forum for men, called Still Fathers (www. stillfathers.org).

Bottling up your emotions isn't healthy, and under such tragic circumstances it really is better to talk things through, both with your partner and with other men. Don't turn your pain and anger inwards, because that's a recipe for self-destruction. You can survive this if you are determined.

It can be easier to accept your loss if you know that you are not alone. For this reason, the rest of this chapter looks at other people's stories.

Andrew's story

In the first pregnancy with our daughter, Rhiannon, everything went well until the final couple of months when my wife developed pre-eclampsia [see p. 42]. I don't think we really understood what this meant and it was never really explained to us. She put on a lot of weight due to fluid retention and ended up in hospital during the last few weeks of her pregnancy.

Eventually the hospital decided they would induce her, but on the day they were due to induce, they took her off all the monitors and sent her home for a bath as there was a shortage of baths at the hospital. During the hour that she was away from the hospital, something happened that constricted the blood flow through the placenta and Rhiannon died.

The hospital then said that my wife had to go through a normal delivery, so she endured the trauma of childbirth knowing that all the pain was for nothing and the baby would be born dead.

The pregnancy triggered a series of auto-immune disorders in my wife, which made her very ill for three years after that. It also saw us embark on a long fight with doctors to pay any attention to the illness, as they repeatedly put her condition down to depression and psychological problems due to Rhiannon's death.

Finally we got a doctor to listen, and it transpired that she was suffering from three very rare auto-immune disorders that, when combined, gave a lot of very random symptoms. After numerous treatments failed, the doctors suggested we try again for a child in the hope that the changes to the immune system brought on by her pregnancy would help her condition.

She soon fell pregnant with our son, and all seemed well until the end of the first trimester when her waters seemed to break – but the pregnancy still held. We then went through a week of randomly waking up at night with the bed soaked in blood as she haemorrhaged and was rushed to hospital, settled down and was then sent home with the pregnancy still intact.

We spent the last trimester at the hospital, but eventually Ross was born three weeks early, but alive. Unfortunately, the loss of fluid in the womb had meant that his lungs weren't fully developed and were incapable of processing enough oxygen. Sadly, a few hours later the doctors pressed me to allow them to shut off his life support, to which I agreed.

After Rhiannon died, I had been in utter shock because we hadn't expected anything to go wrong. In some ways it was worse with Ross, because when I saw him born alive against all odds, I thought everything would be all right. Unfortunately, this built me up for an even bigger fall when I had to take the decision to let him go and switch off the life support.

My wife coped as well she could. She was very sick and relied on the support of both me and her family, to whom she was close. For a while she also turned to spiritualists, horoscopes and fortune tellers, all looking for an answer, but that was short-lived, and done more to search for answers that the doctors simply couldn't supply.

I just couldn't understand how it could have happened to us – twice. My wife and I were always lucky people, so I kept wondering: why us? I also wondered what I had done wrong and how I could have prevented it. We started blaming ourselves, but never each other, but eventually this blame developed into self-loathing which drove a wedge between us. She had gone from being fiercely independent to relying almost totally on me, and over four years this defined our relationship. Then when her health began to improve after Ross was born, she wanted to be independent again and I found myself with no role in the relationship. Combined with our unshared pain, we just drifted apart. This eventually ended in our divorce, not because we no longer loved each other but because, certainly from my side, we no longer loved ourselves, and being together had become too painful.

Mourning them is something that I've never truly been able to do. In both cases, my wife was so ill that I had to shut away a lot of my feelings so I could stay strong for her and help her through when she was often too weak to do anything.

Even today, so many years on, I will be sitting and for no reason their faces will come into my mind, or something daft like a song will trigger a memory of that time and I will fight not to be reduced to tears.

Everyone is concerned for the mother, and no one thinks of the effect it might be having on the man. So I've been uncomfortable talking with anyone about what happened and how it affected me.

Our friends and family felt too embarrassed to talk to me. Instead, all but one of them just ignored me. I've always had an eclectic bunch of friends, and the one from whom I expected the least was the one who gave the most.

He was a bass guitarist and I used to play guitar, so we'd sometimes jam together. He was from a really rough area and none of my other friends would have anything to do with him. But when I was coming home from hospital at 1 a.m. for a few hours' sleep while my wife was going through a long labour with Ross, my friend just happened to be walking by. From then on, he would come in and chat or play guitar, and would let me ramble on or just be silent. He never asked for anything and proved himself the truest friend I had.

I visit Rhiannon's and Ross's graves every year on their birthdays, no matter where I am. No matter where I am in the future, I always will. My work is intensive and I tend to be on call all the time, but they know and my clients know that there are two days in the year when, no matter how big the crises are, I will not allow anyone to contact me. On those days, my ex-wife and I always get together and talk about the past.

Ten years on, I can talk about what happened quite openly, but I never talk about the emotions, not even to my current partner. I don't have any other children, so I don't make a point of talking about Rhiannon and Ross with people, unless they already know.

My feelings surface most often with my family, but when people make stupid remarks it's better not to react. People soon forget what happened as they have their own lives to get on with, and you can't blame them for that.

When my wife and I divorced, I let her keep all the babies' mementoes. I don't need any things to remember them by, because I remember them vividly.

There are a million and one things I would have liked to do differently. I've gone over everything in my head and we did nothing that could have changed the outcome. I do believe our doctors let us down, but what could we have done? You get good and bad doctors wherever you go. I think with Rhiannon, when we found out my wife had pre-eclampsia we should have found out more about the illness rather than blindly trusting the doctors and nurses, but she was our first child and we trusted the medical profession. A pre-eclamptic mother should not be sent home for a bath on the day she is due to be induced; rather, she should be monitored at all times. If this had been done then I am convinced that Rhiannon would still be alive today.

To survive this tragedy together, you have to talk with each other, no matter how painful it is. Understand fully how the other is feeling and help each other through it, but if you can't, then find someone with whom you can talk about it. Don't be tempted to show how strong you are by bottling it up.

Pre-eclampsia affects approximately 10 per cent of pregnancies and usually occurs in the final few weeks, although it can start from the 20th week. It happens when the placenta is damaged, resulting in high blood pressure and swelling for the mother and growth problems for your baby. It requires immediate medical attention. Symptoms include headaches, fuzzy vision, vomiting, swelling and rib pain.

Steve's story

I cope because I have to, though some days I don't want to, I'd rather collapse. Sometimes I want to be where Liam is because I feel he's too small to be on his own.

We've had no counselling and very little support from health professionals, and I'm angry about that. I'm angry at the world. I find myself sometimes wanting confrontation, wanting somebody to say or do the wrong thing so that I can explode. I want to shout at everyone, I want the world to know what happened to our little boy and the pain we suffer every day. Like Kellie, I don't know how to cope. I just do somehow. Some inner strength that I wasn't aware of kicks in and carries me through the dark days. And a good sob helps, too.

Duncan's story

We didn't know that my wife was pregnant until she was five and a half months, and after a few weeks she developed high blood pressure which they brought under control with tablets.

At 37 weeks, we went to the hospital with our two older boys for a routine check-up and when the doctor said she couldn't find our baby's heartbeat, she said it was probably just because he was lying awkwardly. But she sent us to the scan room anyway and that's when our worst fears were realized – our baby son George had died.

My wife was given some tablets to make the birth easier. They told us we would have to come back in three days, but we didn't have to wait that long because she went into labour the next night. Little George was born asleep, weighing 5lb 5oz, with a perfect mop of dark hair.

We were asked if we wanted an autopsy but my wife said she didn't want our baby cut. However, we allowed them to take the placenta and to do some non-invasive tests. When we got the results back all they found wrong were some small blood clots in the placenta, which had stopped the blood flow to George. Otherwise, he was perfectly healthy.

My initial reaction was one of disbelief. How could this happen? I thought I was in a nightmare and I'd wake up and everything would be all right. We couldn't understand why God had taken our son from us, which was funny really, as before I didn't really believe in God, and here I was blaming him for taking our son.

We just wanted a reason, so I read everything I could and I was horrified to find out how many times this happens and that there were so many people in the same situation as us.

On the surface my wife seemed to cope with it better than me, but it was extremely hard both on us and on our two boys, who had been there when we found out. Making all the arrangements for his funeral was awful. I'd never even given anything like this a thought.

On his birthday and at Christmas, I visit the crematorium and put flowers and a card by his plaque. I still find it very hard, and my wife hasn't been back there since we buried his ashes, because she still feels she isn't ready.

I'll always say that I have four sons and one of them is in heaven, because I consider George a part of the family. We've got a book from the hospital with two Polaroid photos, his handprints and footprints, and his tags. My wife also has a locket with some of his hair in it.

My relationship with my wife is much stronger now, even though our 23-year relationship has always been good.

We didn't wait long before trying again, and in October 2003 my wife gave birth to another son, James, who was seven weeks premature and had severe anaemia, but he's OK now. We've just found out she's pregnant again, so that is bringing back memories of our nightmare with George.

Couples have to talk as much as they can about what's happened and not be afraid to cry in front of each other. I've done a lot of that and still do sometimes. Take things at your own pace and try not to be offended by some people's remarks.

Rob's story

We were living in New York during our first pregnancy, which was entirely unremarkable except Rachel's third trimester was marked by the attacks on the Twin Towers. We moved back to England after Thomas was born, and in the summer of 2003 I became chief executive of Bliss, the premature baby charity. Six weeks later, Rachel told me she'd had a positive pregnancy test.

Everything was fine until one Friday evening just before Christmas. Rachel had some bleeding, which was heavy enough for us to go to our local maternity unit. The registrar on duty had a rather cursory look, told us there was little chance it would lead to a miscarriage and sent us home.

On Sunday night, Rachel felt a gush of fluid and realized it was probably her waters breaking. It was a day before her 18th week of pregnancy.

We assumed she was having a miscarriage and the night-duty gynaecologist at the hospital confirmed it. Nevertheless, she sent us home and told us to wait for the contractions to start, at which point we should come back in.

Rachel lost more fluid in the night and we went back in to see the maternity unit the following day. We had a feeling that there might be more to the story than an inevitable miscarriage. This time they admitted Rachel to the hospital for bed rest and observation. They told us that when the waters break at 18 weeks there is a chance that the membranes will close up again and that the amniotic fluid will be replaced over time. One of the midwives on the ward had been through something similar herself and had held the baby in for over 12 weeks after her waters originally broke, giving birth to a healthy baby close to term. So we had reason to hope.

After several spells in hospital interspersed with time spent at home, Rachel carried the baby through Christmas and New Year without going into labour and we were beginning to feel that there might be a real prospect for our baby's survival.

Thomas had visited us in hospital and was there on Christmas Day to open his presents. He knew his mummy wasn't well, but the concept of illness didn't seem really threatening to him and he wouldn't have understood what death was at this stage.

He did worry that his mummy might disappear again and sometimes he still doesn't like it when we go off to hospital for some routine check-up. For six weeks, he saw a lot of me and not much of Rachel, so for a while afterwards it seemed he might have shifted his primary attachment to me.

Working for Bliss, I'd come to learn a lot about premature babies and I knew that if she could hold on until the 28th week, our baby would have a 90 per cent chance of survival. We found out that there was a centre of excellence in Hammersmith which could offer some treatment for Rachel's condition. It involved replacing lost amniotic fluid and seeing if any of it stayed in the uterus.

After several trips there for special scans, we went on 28 January to have the operation. The doctor scanned Rachel one more time to check how the baby was lying, but as soon as she got a clear picture she realized that there was no longer any heartbeat.

Kim, our baby, had died in the womb – only a few hours before the scan, according to what the doctor could tell from his condition. At that stage, he was just a couple of days short of 24 weeks. Had he been born alive there would have been a chance that he'd have survived.

I was very, very sad that Kim had died. I wanted to have him with us so much. I felt very sorry for him since he had struggled hard to stay with us over the past six weeks, but I felt able to accept that he'd not made it. There was a feeling close to pity for his pain, but I was most concerned about Rachel, who had been bravely focusing on the small chance that Kim was going to make it.

I knew his death would devastate her, and what made it worse was that she would have to deliver a dead baby. The following morning, Kim was stillborn at our local maternity hospital.

That was a harrowing experience for both of us, but there were some good points as well. It was a sad but very important experience for me to see our stillborn son lying in a cardboard tray, and we kept him with us for a while. At first I thought I didn't want to see him, but Rachel did. I was glad that she felt that way, because I had such a strong connection to him once I saw him that I realized I would have missed out on an important experience if we'd simply told the nurse to take him away.

Seeing Kim turned him from being a source of fear and unhappiness to being a real person who induced in me a much broader range of emotional responses. This included awe for his beauty and pride about the spirit he had shown fighting for his life.

For the previous six weeks, I'd been focusing on supporting Rachel and organizing the care of our two-year-old. Although many relatives and friends were willing to help, I had to provide the organization to make it all work, including care rotas pinned to our kitchen wall and emailing them to those who were contributing a day or two of their time.

Every day, I was at the hospital, and strangely the time we spent together was wonderful. How often do a mother and father get to spend quiet time with each other for hours, day after day? It was like falling in love again.

After Kim's death, I was very worried about Rachel and made sure that all those around us who needed to be informed were getting their information from me without bothering Rachel. I wanted her to be stress-free, but she was also the only person I really trusted myself to be open with. I could have talked to other people, but I didn't really feel like it.

I could have been devastated or let my world fall apart, but I didn't. I had suffered a loss that hurt, but I have a lot of other things to feel very good about, including Rachel and our little boy Thomas. I felt that others expected me to fall apart, and that when they saw I wasn't they assumed I was going through some kind of unhealthy mental process where I was suppressing my grief. The truth was that I had my sad times, and I still take time to think through my sad thoughts, but they were rarely overwhelming.

We had a funeral for Kim, attended by just myself and Rachel, which was very special. We are putting Kim's name in the memorial book at the local cemetery, along with a plaque. We want to take the opportunity to remember him, and every time we do something along this route we feel sad, but happier for having done it.

I'm still angry at the appalling level of care we received at our local maternity unit and from other medical professionals involved. Some were great, but the rest were bad enough to deserve to be struck off the register. But I'm not angry that fate singled us out to have a very sad experience.

This whole experience has taught us that we should give each other space and support whenever possible. It's a sadness we share, which is a special bond between us.

6

Coping as a couple

Sarah
All this trauma has made my husband and me realize that what we have together is precious. Life is fragile and you need to embrace it. I also think it has made us more tolerant of each other.

Rachel
I had two miscarriages and one stillbirth. When we lost our baby, I had to ring my partner Tony at work to tell him that something was wrong and that the doctors didn't think she was going to survive the birth. Tony was a real support during the actual birth, but afterwards things went wrong.

Tony was devastated too, but dealt with it differently, by becoming tied up in activities to take his mind off what had happened. He was very worried about me because I was in a real state and he had to do everything for our son because I just couldn't manage. He was good at fielding calls, arranging hospital appointments and asking questions for me. But he was worried about money because he's self-employed and obviously wasn't making money if he was home with me, and his grief coupled with his financial worries led to huge rows and resentment.

We fought day and night. I hated him because I thought he didn't love our babies and didn't grieve for them. I wished him dead at times rather than them, and told him that. We got to the point where we seriously considered splitting up. But, with each pregnancy and loss, we grew stronger and were able to lean on each other for support and talk things through. We're 100 times closer now because of what we went through together.

Una
I've had two miscarriages. After the second one my partner burst into tears, but he wouldn't talk about it and failed to acknowledge my pain. Ten days later he was out drinking again with his friends. Sadly, we eventually split up because of it. I didn't have any outside help. I wish I had had bereavement counselling after my first miscarriage, before it got so bad that I left my partner. My friends and family were just as bad. They carried on as if

nothing had happened. My advice? Seek counselling and talk about the loss with your partner. Don't pretend it hasn't happened.

Lynn

I went into labour when I was 26 weeks pregnant. When I got to the hospital, I was told they were very busy and to wait in the visitors' room until someone came to get me. Four hours later no one had come, so my partner lost his temper and caused a scene with the staff. The person who'd told me to wait had gone home without telling anyone I was there. My labour had progressed too far at this point to be stopped, and my baby son was born dreadfully premature.

We were told his chances of survival were only 50–50 and to prepare for the worst. It was a dreadful time for all of us, and my partner didn't want to let any of my family see him in case he died. They were desperate to say hello to him. Miraculously, he was pulling through, feeding through a tube and breathing on his own, until an inexperienced doctor accidentally killed him by piercing his tiny lung with a feeding tube. It was truly awful to think that he'd survived for almost two weeks only to die by the hands that were caring for him.

I was livid, absolutely beside myself with anger. My poor partner coped pretty well at first until doors began shutting in his face at the hospital when no one seemed to want to take the blame. I had depression for a year afterwards and I lost interest in pretty much everything, except for my surviving toddler. On the anniversary of my son's death, we go to his grave, as well as on his birthday, Christmas and Easter. Throughout all this turmoil, my partner and I have managed to keep it together. It could have ripped us apart, but we're stronger than ever.

The loss of your baby might well be the first tragedy you face together as a couple, and you may find yourself exposed to a new side of your partner. In marriage or partnership two become one, but in grief you often become two again, and isolation takes over.

This tragedy can expose weaknesses in an already troubled relationship and can sometimes be the catalyst for a break-up. However, it's a myth that the majority of marriages collapse after the loss of a baby. Although it may be hard to believe in your darkest moment, many parents say their experience has proved a source of tremendous personal growth, and has helped them form a special new bond with their partner. Many couples become closer as they learn more about each other's sensitivities and strengths.

The stress of grieving can make you so introspective and needy that you may find it hard to support each other, and it may be hard to find any energy left over to care for each other. But, even if he doesn't always show it, your partner probably needs your help and understanding in order to express his feelings, while you might need his help and support in completing practical tasks and getting your life back on track.

If you are grieving in different ways, as many couples do, it can be hard to empathize with your partner's way of coping. This is a shared trauma – releasing your feelings to each other will help relieve some of the pain, and just knowing that you can rely upon your partner not to judge you can bring you closer together. The keys to making sure your relationship survives are: accepting your differences, continuing communication, and reassuring one another.

Do men and women grieve differently?

Some experts believe that if a loss occurs during pregnancy, a woman traditionally takes it harder than her partner because she feels closer to the baby, whereas a man tends not to bond with his child until after the birth. This may be true to a certain extent, but this way of thinking can also be very divisive. It's not a competition to see which of you is more justified in their grief, depending on the strength of your bond with your baby.

Tina
Paul couldn't understand how hurt I was, as he never felt pregnant. With my ectopic pregnancy, I feel guilty because *I* signed the forms to have the operation that ended it. He just sees it that I had to have the op or I would have died. He doesn't see the baby as ever having been viable, whereas to me it was my child and I killed it.

Claire
When we lost Adam, my partner was in tears, totally shocked. When he told our relatives, apparently he was heartbroken. He was a fantastic support. He struggled as much as I did, but it went

unnoticed because he had to be strong and talk to people, as I was not up to it. He took over a lot of jobs that I usually do.

No two people grieve in exactly the same way and on the same schedule. But in addition, misunderstanding can stem from the belief that men and women grieve differently, with women being seen as more open and readier to express their feelings, while men are generally viewed as more reserved.

In fact, grief is the same no matter what your gender. Studies indicate that, after one month of a loss, both men and women experience the same level of pain, yearning and crying. But, while men and women suffer the same actual experience of the loss, there are differences in the freedom with which they express their grief, and there are some generally recognized gender differences in grieving patterns. Men in our culture are conditioned not to show their emotions – apart from a good outburst of anger – and so may appear to dismiss them, perhaps coping by taking refuge in work or other activities: Rachel's partner dealt with his grief by plunging into work, Una's by drinking with his friends. Many men also feel the need to appear strong for their partner's sake, fearing that she won't be able to cope if he does break down and show feelings – something which again may be misunderstood as indifference. In fact, many men are more likely to grieve in private.

It wasn't until several months after Tina's ectopic pregnancy that she learned how guilty her partner Paul felt because he hadn't been able to protect her from the pain she had suffered. He also felt guilty and helpless at the fact that she had had to go through the physical side of it alone. Tina did have the chance to talk to Paul about his feelings, though well after the event. 'I just wish he had told me at the time,' Tina said.

Another problem is a special kind of male isolation, when attention may be focused on the woman while the man is ignored. In addition, he may not have any friends he feels he can turn to. In this case, he may well be feeling wounded and alone, and may need someone to ask him how he's feeling – and be genuinely interested in his answer.

Tina

No one asked Paul how he was, except me. He was brought up to 'be a man' and that it is weak to show your feelings. He was obviously sad about losing the babies, but never showed it, though he became very protective of me.

Some research suggests that most fathers resolve or make peace with their grief in three to six months, while most mothers need nine to 24 months or more. This kind of generalization is fairly meaningless; as bereaved parents know, the grief from losing a child never goes away. However, it does show the kind of thinking and expectations that centre around men and their grief. My advice is to ignore them, and to respect the pace of your own individual grief, and that of your partner.

You may also need to ignore gender stereotypes as you grieve – the strong, silent man and the verbal woman may be hopelessly wrong for you if you, the woman, often prefer to keep your counsel while your man is more verbally communicative.

Learning to respect each other's grieving styles may in fact prove a source of strength. For example, the partner who has trouble expressing emotion (whether that's the man or the woman) or who tends to run away from it, can benefit by listening to the more open partner who is more consciously focused on grief. Sharing different insights and moments of faith can strengthen the other. Opposites not only attract; they may also help each other to heal.

Keep communicating

Kate
My partner bottled up his grief, as men do, although he managed not to let me push him away, which is why we are still together now eight years down the road. But getting him to communicate his emotions is still like getting blood out of a stone.

You may find it hard to express your feelings and to muster the strength to talk, but talking honestly is one of the best routes through your grief. Your partner can't read your mind, and that goes for both men and women. Tell your partner how you are feeling, otherwise he might make incorrect assumptions which lead to misunderstandings. Do allow for the fact that both of you are feeling more vulnerable now than usual – perhaps more ready to fly off the handle, or more acutely sensitive to any suspicion of neglect or coldness.

It can be hard just to listen to your partner without offering a solution, but this may be all that's required for the time being. Let him know that the best way to help is to let you talk first and then empathize with you, rather than jumping in with platitudes or 'solutions'. There may be feelings of anger you need to express, and your partner might misinterpret this as you blaming him. Again, let him know that this is not the case. Once you've expressed your feelings and talked about them realistically, they often lose their destructive potential.

Some couples do feel a need to apportion blame. Sometimes it is just human nature to look for someone to blame the event on – one reason why the bereaved often blame medical personnel for a loved one's death, even when they are not at fault. For example, you might perhaps want to blame your partner for not driving you to the hospital fast enough, or not being sufficiently assertive with the staff there. He might feel you are to blame for not taking better care of yourself in pregnancy, for example not getting enough rest or having an alcoholic drink, even though rationally you both know that none of your actions actually affected your pregnancy. You might also need to discuss feelings of betrayal by others – doctors and other authority figures, or family or friends who you feel have let you down with lack of attention or insensitive remarks. Again, these feelings may need to be talked through more than once before they can be resolved.

To avoid blaming each other, try and keep the focus on your own feelings when talking. Use 'I' messages – e.g. 'I feel upset when I think you're switching off . . . not listening . . .' It may also help to admit empathy: for example, 'I understand that you feel angry.' Acknowledging his feelings may help your partner to open up more easily. This is possible even when you're not getting on well.

Louise

Louis' father and I had split up just before we found out I was pregnant, but we shared the two days of our baby's life and a lot of time together afterwards. I couldn't bear to be alone. We helped each other through the first few months, and felt as if it was only the two of us who understood and felt the loss equally. We've had our ups and downs, but we're friends. I think I would have found grieving more difficult if I'd been totally alone. But I've also been able to deal with it in my own way, without the pressures of an ongoing relationship with a partner.

Communicating is more than talking. Having a good cry together is also a route through your grief – painful, indeed, but often more healing than not crying. You may find that you are crying for other matters than the baby, such as changes in your expectations of each other, or the loss of earlier dreams about your relationship. Don't worry. It is natural for many feelings of loss to surface at such a time. Life has changed irrevocably, but new life is always growing behind the pain, and there is a good, strong future for your relationship if you want it.

Writing is another way of communicating. If you're having trouble hearing each other out, pour out your emotions to each other in a letter, note or email. That way there are no interruptions and you can take the time to properly think about what your partner has said before you react.

Sex, the ultimate communication, can be a confused issue at such a time. Men may look for reassurance through sex, whereas you may be too tense or feel too guilty, and would prefer something safer, like hugs and cuddles. Let your partner know this, so neither one of you feels pressured into doing something that your heart's not in. A simple way of remaining connected with your partner is non-sexual touching, like a back-rub or a foot massage. It can open you up to more honest conversation.

Kate
Initially I tried to push my partner away and we went through hell. I was angry he wasn't there when I had the twins and I was angry he didn't beat up the medical staff. I was angry he didn't make the decision to take some time off work. Despite it all, we're still together and have three gorgeous boys so I am really lucky. I would never swap my life for anyone else's. Everyone grieves differently, but I found you have to spend lots of time together and talk!

What you can do

Some research shows that couples who make a conscious resolution to get through their grief together have a better chance of keeping their relationships intact than couples who don't make any such decision. So perhaps the main thing you can do is jointly to decide that together you will weather this.

Don't let your relationship crumble over this. It might be a struggle, and sometimes you might question whether it's worth it, but if you had a good relationship before, don't let it slip away.

Remember why you fell in love in the first place and the good times you've had together. You can come out of this tragedy stronger and closer.

If this is your first close experience of death, as happens with many couples, you need to make allowances for this, too. You may be totally unprepared and very frightened. It is by no means uncommon to fear that something may happen to you, too. Your usual friends and activities may drop away and be of little help. There is a divide between your life before and after your first experience of death, so do allow for those feelings of fear and vulnerability, as well as the very special grief you are experiencing.

Get support

Studies on resilience show that people are better able to cope with adversity if they have the strong support of family and friends. Likewise, couples that surround themselves with supportive people are more likely to stay together than those who try to do it alone. Spending time with other bereaved parents, especially those who underwent a loss earlier than you, can also be comforting.

Spend time together

If one or both of you doesn't feel like talking, don't force it. Just being together may help. One study showed that 90 per cent of both men and women surveyed found that being alone with their partners helped them cope with grief. You can share feelings in silence on a long walk. Sometimes, too, it is easier to talk when one or both of you is occupied with an activity such as gardening or fishing.

Consider counselling

An impartial third person can be a great source of support when both you and your partner are still very raw. Counselling may also help some men express feelings that they may have been bottling up. Some couples take refuge in silence in an attempt to avoid hurting each other, and sometimes it feels safer to express pain if there's a third party to provide support to both of you. If one partner doesn't want counselling, it can still help the other, so don't be pressurized by counsellors who insist that both of you must come along. If even one partner does decide to see a counsellor, it may free the other partner to face the same challenge, or to take other steps in dealing with grief.

Find some way of remembering your child together

Creating a memorial for your child can provide an outlet for the type of grief that needs to express itself in activity. Working on this together can help maintain closeness. This could be something simple like creating a special area of the garden, or starting a memorial fund for the condition from which your child died.

Rachel and her partner visit their three daughters' graves and light a candle on each of their birthdays (the babies suffered a genetic condition incompatible with life, Jeune syndrome). See Chapter 2, 'Saying goodbye', for more ideas on memorials.

7

Telling your other children

Claire
I already had two beautiful children when I became pregnant with Adam. Everything was fine until I reached 30 weeks, when I had protein in my water. I was admitted to hospital, monitored for 24 hours, then discharged. I was re-admitted several other times – I fell, and then had high blood pressure. The longer I was pregnant, the less movement I was feeling, but as soon as I made a trip to hospital he'd move, so I'd get sent home again.

On my last fateful trip to hospital, I was in labour and walking up and down the corridor to help Adam move down. I was six centimetres dilated at this point. When I met my midwife in the corridor, I had a really strong contraction and she helped me breathe through it. When she came back to check on Adam's heartbeat, she couldn't find one. I started to panic and then all these consultants started hurrying in. They rushed me into the scanning room and found his heart had stopped beating. I just kept screaming, 'No, no, no! What happened? What am I going to tell my girls?'

What do you tell the children? And should you tell them at all? The general answer to the latter question would seem to be yes. Hard as it is to talk to children about death, most parents who have experienced the death of a baby agree that it is even harder to keep silent about the event, and that it is important to be open with their children about what has happened. The key fact to face is that you all need to grieve. Clear, simple, truthful explanations are best, because it will help them grieve.

If you hide death from your children, it's something they will learn to fear and develop out-of-proportion thoughts about. But if you let them go through the grieving process with you, they will develop a more realistic view.

Claire
My girls were so excited about their little baby brother coming home. My parents tried to carry on normally with them, hard as it

was. All day in hospital we were torn between wanting to get home to the girls to tell them about Adam and wanting to stay with Adam. I didn't know what to say to them. When we set off back home, we warned my parents that we were five minutes away, and they had them in their bath, so I was ready and composed about what I was going to tell them. They came rushing down the stairs, saying, 'Adam, Adam!' but as soon as they reached the door, they just stopped and looked at us. My five-year-old just hugged her nanny and my youngest, who was three, asked where Adam was. I broke the news to them then, using the memory book that the hospital had made for us. I told my five-year-old the truth as much as we knew ourselves, saying that Adam was a poorly baby when he was born and wasn't able to breathe, so he died. I showed her the picture of Adam, with his purple lips, and explained why they were that colour.

I told them that we were all going to be very sad for a long time and that the angels had left us a special story with his picture and prints, and that whenever we wanted to talk to Adam, we just had to look up at the night sky and the star that was twinkling was Adam. I told my youngest a simpler version, and they had a good cry with us.

Your other children will need plenty of reassurance and love from you to come to terms with the event. But, if you are open and honest and provide age-appropriate explanations, they too will come to terms with what has happened.

Including your children

Your children may find it easier to cope if you include them in preparations for a funeral or remembrance service. Most younger children need to see things tangibly before they can understand, so, contrary to what many people will tell you, it may be best not to leave them out of the funeral or memorial service. Explain to them beforehand what will happen that day and listen to their suggestions about what to include in the ceremony. Getting them to write a little poem and draw something to be put in the coffin will make them feel more included, and if they're old enough they can perhaps do a reading as well.

Jane

Our three living children (who were then eight, seven and five) took part in the funeral preparations. They each picked out some flowers for Laura's bouquet and wrote her cards saying that they would always love and miss her.

We continue to honour our baby's memory as a family and have always included our youngest son (who was born almost a year after our daughter was stillborn) in our rituals of remembrance. (Ian made his first visit to Laura's grave when he was just two weeks of age, in fact.)

Family support at this time can be important for your other children – another reason for allowing them to attend the funeral. Children can be very sensitive to feelings of being excluded from a family secret, and being surrounded by family members will help reassure and comfort them.

Explaining death and dealing with fears

This may be your other children's first real experience of death, and it may be difficult for them to understand why the baby can't simply come back. Very young children in particular tend to think that death is reversible and the baby will return. They'll be confused and feel overwhelmed at the intensity of their emotions. Any disruption to their routine can be unsettling, so try to keep some of their regular activities going, and continue normal patterns of discipline – boundaries provide reassurance too. Get friends and family to help, so the burden isn't on you when you don't feel like facing the outside world.

You know your other children best yourself, so will know just how much to explain, but here are a few suggestions.

Very young children

Children up to the age of four or five may not understand death but can and do still grieve. Younger children often find it difficult to describe how they're feeling, and the effects may show in non-verbal cues and changes of behaviour such as disrupted sleep, regression to baby talk, thumb-sucking, bedwetting, inability to concentrate on schoolwork, difficulty in sleeping, nightmares, aggression, separation anxiety, sulking and reluctance to talk. Some of these are attention-seeking behaviours or just signals that they need your care, so don't judge them too harshly.

Questions you might be faced with include: 'When is the baby coming back?' 'Can we get the baby from hospital now?', 'When will the baby wake up?' and 'Where is the baby?' You can say: 'Being dead means we can't see the baby again.'

Try and answer questions as they come, but no more; if your child wants to know more, he or she will probably ask. Do also allow for children 'switching off' from grief or explanations when they've had enough – for example, a child who's been sitting on your lap having a deep chat may suddenly run off to play, and will be found deeply immersed in a new game while you're still wondering how to answer her next question. In fact, play is an important way of coping with grief, through make-believe games or through artwork such as drawing or modelling.

It is also quite common for a young child to believe that he or she has somehow caused the death of the baby, either through some action such as throwing a tantrum or breaking a toy, or simply through magical thinking, such as wishing the new arrival away through jealousy. If your child had been apprehensive about the new arrival, thinking it would monopolize your affections, they may be feeling guilty and worried that they *made* the baby meet its death. They may also be scared to tell you this. Do ask your children about any concerns or fears they may have, so you can reassure them and give them a rational, but simple, explanation – their fears may appear absurd to an adult but are very real to them.

If your child is in primary school, they'll have a better grasp of death and understand that it's final, but they may think that someone else has caused the death. They may also think that death is contagious, and not want to be left alone in case you go away too.

There is one way of dealing with unfinished business which I think is very effective. Sit them down with a picture of their dead baby sister or brother and get them to talk to it, saying everything that is on their mind, both good and bad. It helps them work towards closure on the worst of their grief.

School-age children

Children who have reached school age may have specific questions to ask about the details of death, what happens to a body after death, and the funeral and cremation processes. This interest can sometimes appear a little macabre to outsiders, but is all part of the way that children learn about the reality of death.

Older children may indeed take on the reality of death too well, and may be anxious about the possibility of other family members dying, or may worry about their own mortality. They may be extra sensitive to anyone getting the slightest illness, such as a cough or cold, fearing that any illness automatically leads to death, so do also explain clearly the difference between the baby's problems and common illnesses like the flu. They may well think that since the baby went away, then you'll go away too. This fear of abandonment is very common, so reassure them that you're not going anywhere.

The older your child is, the more realistic an understanding he or she will have of what being dead actually means, so you may find yourself being asked quite esoteric or philosophical questions about life and death. Bear in mind that even slightly older children, with a developed sense of what's right and wrong, might still think that death is a punishment. They'll also be mourning the loss of any personal relationship they'd hoped for with their new baby brother or sister.

Encourage them to express their feelings in the coming weeks and months through drawing and writing. They need to know it's all right to be feeling the way they do, as long as they're not being destructive. No matter how angry they get, you have to be firm with them about violence of any kind being unacceptable, so give them more acceptable ways of venting their rage, such as taking exercise or punching a pillow.

- Be truthful.
- Keep it simple and explain it in their language, e.g. 'The baby was born too soon and his body didn't work.'
- Try and find out early on if other children feel they are to blame for their sibling's death, and explain that wishing a new baby away does not cause a death, neither do feelings of jealousy.
- Explain to them that it is their sibling's death that has made you feel very sad, not anything they may have done.
- Include them in your grieving process and allow them to see you cry, and to cry with you if need be. They may need to know it's all right to cry too.
- Do talk about the dead child – it helps everyone.
- Be careful how you phrase explanations. Young children can misinterpret or take things literally. For example, if you say, 'Mummy lost the baby,' your children may wonder why you're not looking for him and ask if they can help in the search.
- Painful though it is, it's probably best to use the word 'dead'. If you say, 'Mummy's baby went to sleep,' your children may think

that the baby will wake up sometime soon, or they may be afraid to go to sleep in case the same thing happens to them.

- Comfort each other. Grief is hard work and very tiring, and both you and your other children need all the comfort you can get. Don't stint on simple measures such as extra physical contact – more hugs and cuddles, or allowing the child into your bed at night.

Seeing the baby

Claire
There are a lot of regrets that we both have as parents, such as not bathing my little baby son, not getting him dressed, not giving him a blanket to snuggle up in his casket with – things I just never thought of at the time. Sometimes I also regret not letting the girls see their brother. My eldest sometimes says she wishes she had seen Adam and had given him a kiss and cuddle before he went to heaven.

If you allow your other children to view your dead baby, bear in mind that, to them, the baby will probably look as if he or she is asleep, hence perhaps leading them to equate sleep with death. You can explain that all mummies, daddies and children sleep every day, as otherwise they wouldn't be able to work or play the next day because they would be tired. However, you may need to explain that even though their sibling appears to be asleep, his or her heart has in fact stopped because it was broken or not working properly, and the baby won't be able to wake up. Repetition is the key here for this message to sink in (along with reassurance that going to sleep is quite safe).

8

Complementary therapies for grief

Working through your grief isn't just about the passage of time. It's about living through your emotions, and for some people this can lead into new paths and a journey of self-discovery.

Complementary therapies may help you cope with your grief and improve your health, and hence your chances of future conception. More immediately, they may help you heal in body and mind – and this can be important given that some women develop a mistrust or fear of their body after losing a baby. Complementary therapists look at you as a whole person and try to understand the link between your mind and body's health. Some of the women and men interviewed for this book said they felt poorly treated by the medical professionals involved, feeling that they lacked tact and compassion. This may be the unfortunate result of our healthcare system being pushed to the limit. Certainly, a complementary therapist may be able to give you more time and attention than is usually possible in a conventional medical setting.

British consumers spend £130 million annually on complementary therapies, and this is expected to rise to £200 million by 2008. One in every two Britons has now visited an alternative health practitioner. The industry is shaking off its 'quack' image as more research is published on the effectiveness of various treatments.

The National Institute for Clinical Excellence (NICE), which is part of the NHS and is responsible for producing guidelines for treatment, is currently studying research on the effectiveness and safety of complementary therapies. This would allow those therapies meeting nationwide standards to be made available on the NHS. However, they will be using the strictest possible elimination methods so that only watertight, scientifically proven therapies are recommended. Many of the following therapies may not meet their standards. However, each of them has a long history of helping emotions relating to grief and bereavement.

You may not have tried a complementary therapy before or may be sceptical of it, but it wouldn't be so popular if it didn't work. For more information, try reading the monthly magazine *Natural Health*. Read on to find out which therapy may suit your needs.

Acupuncture

What is it?

A technique based on the principle that your health is dependent on your body's energy, or Qi, flowing freely through a series of channels in your body.

How does it work?

By inserting very fine needles into these channels, your therapist can remove blockages and restore your natural balance. Don't worry if you hate needles and getting shots because the needles used are so very fine that you'll hardly feel anything at all, and it's most certainly not a painful experience.

What is it good for?

The flow of Qi can be disturbed by a number of factors including anger, anxiety, grief, stress, poor nutrition, infections, trauma and over-exertion.

Length of treatment?

Your first session will be longer than subsequent ones, about an hour. It lets your therapist determine your general state of health and medical history, in order to identify where your blockages are.

How much does it cost?

First sessions lasting an hour generally cost from £25 and follow-up sessions from £20.

Where do I find a local practitioner?

The British Acupuncture Council
63 Jeddo Road
London W12 9HQ
Tel: 020 8735 0400
Website: www.acupuncture.org.uk
Email: info@acupuncture.org.uk

Aromatherapy

What is it?

The healing use of oils extracted from plants. The oils are produced from flowers, seeds, fruits, leaves, bark and roots, preferably from organically grown plants. The practice dates back to ancient Egypt.

How does it work?

The oils are most commonly used in oil burners, inhalation treatments, massage and baths. They are absorbed through your skin's pores, entering your bloodstream before targeting your nervous system. Although they're safe to use at home, you must NEVER put neat oils directly on to your skin. They must be mixed with a carrier oil, like almond or grapeseed. It's recommended that you see a practitioner the first time you decide to use aromatherapy oils. They'll ask you about your current health and lifestyle, as well as any specific emotion you want to target, so they can tailor a blend of oils for you before massaging them into your skin. Always drink lots of water afterwards, as the elimination of toxins will make you feel dehydrated.

What is it good for?

The best oils to try for grief are:

- *clary sage*: good for tension and panic attacks;
- *frankincense*: helps relieve stress and nervous tension;
- *geranium*: helps mood swings and anxiety;
- *grapefruit*: a really uplifting mood-booster and stimulant;
- *jasmine*: improves self-confidence and is emotionally comforting;
- *lavender*: soothing and relaxing;
- *lemon*: eases depression, confusion and anxiety;
- *mandarin*: good for nervous tension;
- *palmarosa*: helps clear your mind;
- *valerian*: eases restlessness and nervous tension;
- *ylang ylang*: a brilliant anti-depressant.

Length of treatment?

Your first appointment normally lasts one hour, and subsequent visits are up to personal preference.

How much does it cost?

Upwards of £35 for an appointment. Individual oils for home use start from £2 at your local health food store.

Where do I find a local practitioner?

The International Federation of Aromatherapists
182 Chiswick High Road
London W4 1PP

Tel: 020 8742 2605
Website: www.ifaroma.org
Email: office@ifaroma.org

Emotional freedom technique (EFT)

What is it?

A form of psychological acupressure, based on the same energy channels used in traditional acupuncture (see p. 64), but without the use of needles. It's based on the belief that a traumatic event or situation causes a disruption in your body's energy system and emotional wellbeing.

How does it work?

The therapist will tap with their fingertips to input kinetic energy to specific points on your head and upper torso, while you focus on your problem. By targeting and clearing this disruption using EFT, your pain caused by the trauma is relieved.

What is it good for?

Anxiety, stress, tension, bereavement, headaches and migraines, post-traumatic stress disorder, insomnia, panic attacks, phobias, poor self-esteem and confidence, guilt and pain.

Length of treatment?

Your situation can often be treated in just one gentle session, with lasting results, and you can also learn how to apply the techniques to yourself at home. So it's fast, effective, painless and convenient.

How much does it cost?

One-hour sessions start from £35

Where do I find a local practitioner?

The Healer Foundation
Sunday School House
The Village
Thurstonland
Huddersfield
West Yorkshire HD4 6XX

Tel: 01484 664 069
Email: rena.g@virgin.net

Herbalism

What is it?
The medicinal use of plants and herbs. It dates back thousands of years to Tibetan monks.

How does it work?
It's a holistic approach to health. Plants with a particular affinity for certain organs or systems of the body are used to 'feed' and restore to health those parts that have become weakened. As the body is strengthened so is its power and ability to fight off disease, and when balance and harmony are restored, health will be regained. Capsules, compresses, infusions and tinctures are the most common forms.

What is it good for?
Insomnia, stress, headaches and migraines.

Length of treatment?
Your initial appointment will last between an hour and an hour and a half. Your practitioner should take your full medical history and, after an initial examination, prescribe a course of herbs and give you guidelines on how to use them. Subsequent visits will usually be 30 minutes.

How much does it cost?
Expect to pay anything between £20 and £50 per session, including the herbs.

Where do I find a local practitioner?
The National Institute of Medical Herbalists
Elm House
54 Mary Arches Street,
Exeter EX4 3BA
Tel: 01392 426 022
Website: www.nimh.org.uk
Email: nimh@ukexeter.freeserve.co.uk

Homeopathy

What is it?

Homeopathy means 'similar' (*homeos*) 'suffering' (*pathos*). It treats the person as a whole, rather than just the body or condition, and takes into account all the symptoms – physical, mental and emotional. There are three important laws in homeopathy: your symptoms move from the top of your body downwards, internally to externally, and from your most important organs to your least important.

How does it work?

Based on the belief that 'like cures like', minute quantities of remedies are used which in massive doses produce effects similar to those of the condition being treated. Remedies with as little as one molecule per million can stimulate the body's healing mechanism. The cause of the problem is treated, rather than just the symptoms, so that the body's defence system is strengthened and your general wellbeing improves.

What is it good for?

Shock, stress and insomnia. The best remedies for grief are:

- *aconite*: for the shock of sudden death, especially if you're hysterical;
- *arnica*: if you receive sudden bad news but claim to be perfectly in control;
- *ignatia*: good for loss of emotional control, rapid mood swings and hysteria;
- *pulsatilla*: if you're very weepy and want constant attention;
- *nux vom*: if you're in denial, angry and even violent;
- *natrum mur*: if you're turning inwards and don't want to talk to anyone, as well as annual recurrences of grief on the anniversary of your loss.

Length of treatment?

Although you can now buy homeopathic remedies at your local pharmacy, it's best to have an initial consultation with a trained homeopath, so you can get the best remedy to suit your needs. The homeopath will ask you what your main complaint is, and will go through your medical history, diet and lifestyle before they recommend a remedy or several remedies to be used together. Generally, your remedy will be in the 30c potency and to be taken three times a day. This is reduced as your symptoms improve.

How much does it cost?

A consultation costs from £30. Individual remedies in a 7g vial, containing approximately 70 tablets, will cost between £3.50 and £5.50.

Where do I find a local practitioner?

The British Homeopathic Association
Hahnemann House
29 Park Street West
Luton LU1 3BE
Tel: 0870 444 3950
Website: www.trusthomeopathy.org

Neuro-linguistic programming (NLP)

What is it?

NLP is the study of achievement or success. 'Neuro' refers to how the mind and body interact, 'linguistic' refers to the insights that can be obtained by paying attention to your use of language, and 'programming' refers to the study of thinking and behavioural patterns.

How does it work?

You're taught a new way of thinking so that you communicate more effectively and have stronger personal relationships. It can help you to: become less stressed and upset; argue less; repair friendships; avoid saying things you don't mean and then regret; avoid leaving people frustrated with you and you with them; get rid of irrational behaviour.

What is it good for?

Traumatic memories, grief and loss, stress, depression, guilt, relaxation, self-development, anxiety, confidence-building, anger and getting rid of negative thought patterns and behaviours.

Length of treatment?

Usually weekend courses and workshops.

How much does it cost?

Workshops start from £125, but vary widely

Where do I find a local practitioner?

Professional Guild of NLP
PO Box 104
Clitheroe
Lancashire BB7 9ZG
Tel: 0845 226 7334
Website: www.professionalguildofnlp.com
Email: info@professionalguildofnlp.com

Reflexology

What is it?

A practice originating in China over 5,000 years ago, based on the principle that all your body's energy is grounded in your feet.

How does it work?

The therapist uses pressure points, mostly on your feet but sometimes on your hands, which correspond to very specific parts of your body, to stimulate your body's own healing power and correct any imbalances in you. It's one of the complementary therapies more widely available on the NHS.

What is it good for?

Reducing stress and tension, relieving fatigue and eliminating toxins from your body.

Length of treatment?

One hour. Your therapist will ask you questions about your medical history, as well as your lifestyle, especially your diet, exercise and stress levels. You'll then be asked to take off your shoes and socks and your therapist will test your reflex points for any tenderness or sensitivity, which indicates stuck or blocked energy. The sensation may take some getting used to, as they will be pressing quite firmly, but it shouldn't ever be painful. It's also important that you drink plenty of water after your treatment to help flush out the toxins.

How much does it cost?

Between £35 and £40.

Where do I find a local practitioner?

The Association of Reflexologists
27 Old Gloucester Street,
London WC1N 3XX
Tel: 0870 567 3320
Website: www.aor.org.uk
Email: info@aor.org.uk

Reiki

What is it?

An ancient form of healing by touch. 'Rei' means universal and 'ki' means life energy.

How does it work?

The practitioner channels this energy through their hands, to encourage your body to heal, both physically and emotionally. This stimulates positive changes in your attitude, so that you become happier.

What is it good for?

Relief of stress and tension, and improvement in personal relation-ships.

Length of treatment?

Usually one hour, but can be 30 minutes. During a treatment, you'll lie fully clothed while the therapist's hands lightly touch you, focusing on your main energy centres, or charkas. It's so gentle you might not even feel their hands on you.

How much does it cost?

Starts from £25.

Where do I find a local practitioner?

UK Reiki Federation
PO Box 1785
Andover SP11 OWB

Tel: 01264 773 774
Website: www.reikifed.co.uk
Email: enquiry@reikifed.co.uk

Traditional Chinese medicine (TCM)

What is it?

An ancient holistic healing system that focuses on re-establishing balance and harmony in your body, by restoring the flow of Qi (vital energy), and the balance of yin and yang (the opposite but complementary forces encompassing the whole of life). It's one of the most well-established and scientifically proven complementary therapies in the West. Although we consider it complementary, it's actually the primary healthcare system used by 20 per cent of the world's population!

How does it work?

TCM therapists use acupuncture, heat application (moxibustion), herbal preparations, massage, meditation, diet therapy and exercises, such as tai chi and qigong.

What is it good for?

Stress, anger, depression, general confusion, migraine and pain.

Length of treatment?

Your first visit will usually last one and a half hours and will include a full consultation and diagnosis, along with a session of acupuncture, acupressure or massage. You will be asked about your medical history, as well as your lifestyle, sleep patterns and current emotions. Then your tongue will be examined for its structure, colour and coating, your voice and breathing patterns listened to, and your pulse taken. The course of treatment will be tailored around whether you have an excess of Qi (so you need to be calmed) or a Qi deficiency (so you need to be boosted). If you're also prescribed a course of Chinese herbs, then these will come either as pills or in a loose mixture that you will brew like tea.

How much does it cost?

Your first appointment will cost from £25 and doesn't include the price of any Chinese herbs prescribed. Follow-up appointments will usually last 30 minutes and cost from £13.

Where do I find a local practitioner?

Chinese Medical Institute and Register (UK)
103–105 Camden High Street,
London NW1 7JN
Tel: 020 7388 6704

Yoga

What is it?

Stretching exercises to improve the union of your mind and body. It's been practised in India for over 5,000 years and today almost half a million Britons practise it.

How does it work?

The physical aim is to increase your flexibility, while the spiritual aim is to relieve stress and counter any negative emotions. There are many different types of yoga classes available, so ask your instructor which one they are using. Also, ask what their qualifications are: there are a lot of fitness instructors who claim to be yoga teachers, but if they don't talk you through the correct posture and breathing, as well as the emotive aspect, then you're just attending a glorified stretch-and-tone class.

What is it good for?

Insomnia, lack of concentration, stress and aggression.

Length of treatment?

Each class will normally last an hour or more. It will start with a gentle warm-up before your teacher leads you through a series of asanas, or poses. You could do all this at home with a video, but it's important that you have someone correcting your poses when you begin.

How much does it cost?

Part of your gym membership; group classes held in a community centre generally cost £5; one-on-one tuition costs from £40.

Where do I find a local practitioner?

British Wheel of Yoga
25 Jermyn Street,
Sleaford

Lincolnshire NG34 7RU
Tel: 01529 306 851
Website: www.bwy.org.uk
Email: information@bwy.org.uk

9

Planning for another baby

It takes courage to start planning for another baby after losing one or more through miscarriage, stillbirth or infant death. I say 'planning for' rather than 'trying again' as 'trying' perhaps implies that perhaps you did not try hard enough last time, with unfortunate connotations of 'must try harder' – quite out of place in an event where one of the key feelings was probably the frightening sense that events were not in your control.

You now have intimate knowledge of what is rarely discussed in the usual ante-natal preparations today – the vulnerability of new life, and how easily it can be blotted out. You may be wondering if you're fated or singled out in some way for another loss, especially if you've already experienced more than one loss. While, statistically, the death of a baby can happen to any pregnant woman or new mother, for you it's real and creates very sharp fears of what may happen this time round. You may feel pulled in opposite directions – one being not to waste any time and get pregnant, the other to play it safe and not take the chance that your loss can happen again.

Kate
We decided to try for another baby quite soon after, and within four months I was pregnant again with our little boy, Llewi, who is now nine months. Admittedly, I became very obsessed with having another baby. I know he's not a substitute, but I felt there was a big void in my life. Conceiving him was easy – it was getting through this pregnancy that was difficult because I was always worried that something else was going to go wrong.

Knowing when you're ready

No matter how much time passes after the loss, the decision to plan for another pregnancy is difficult. As all bereaved parents know, there is no question that having another baby will erase the pain of your loss, or 'replace' the baby who has gone, no matter how strong you feel your need is to get pregnant.

But how do you *really* know when you're ready? This is a personal decision, and there is no one right answer. For some women, the way is obvious – they won't be happy until they're pregnant again. They may still decide to wait a while, however, for emotional or physical reasons. Others may feel that they may need more time, or simply that they can't yet begin to consider another pregnancy. No matter where you are in the stages of decision, each is individual and should be respected as such.

As you well know, becoming pregnant again is far more than a physical event; it is a whole new life adventure. Embarking on this challenge means you will have to cope with milestones such as the first scan, the first trimester and the first movements of your baby.

This can mean living through the paradox of still grieving for your first baby while celebrating new life. So the emotions of a subsequent pregnancy may well be more complex than those of an earlier one.

There are advantages both to waiting and to getting pregnant soon after the loss of your baby. Waiting will allow you more time to heal physically and emotionally and may help you feel less anxious during the pregnancy. Getting pregnant sooner may make you feel you're leaving the painful past behind and moving on with life.

Do you *feel* ready, both physically and emotionally? Deep down you've got to ask yourself if you are truly 'over' your loss – for example, if you cry every time you think about your baby, then perhaps you're not really emotionally ready to plan for another. You have to be strong enough to be able to deal with a new life adventure with all its emotional and physical challenges – yet you may not know whether you are strong enough until you actually go ahead. It will make you much less anxious if you are able to make peace with your grief before your next pregnancy, but sometimes the only way you can become ready is to go ahead and become pregnant.

Donna
My next pregnancy wasn't as frightening as I expected it to be. The baby was much more active and I felt him move early, but I was continually worried that I'd miscarry so I only truly relaxed once I got past seven months. My GP and midwives were brilliant – I never went more than two weeks without being monitored.

Points to consider before conceiving

Your health
You may well find that you are physically ready to plan for another baby before you are emotionally ready. The general rule is to wait

until you have had at least one to two periods to strengthen the chance of a healthy pregnancy. Research suggests that the risk of miscarriage in the next pregnancy is about one and a half times higher if you don't allow yourself one normal cycle before you try again.

However, many health professionals suggest that you should wait between three and six months or even up to a year. How long to wait does vary according to the individual, and many factors are involved – emotional considerations, the reason your last pregnancy ended, your age, and so on. Your body may need time to heal after a miscarriage, especially if you've had surgical procedures. You may also need to wait longer if you have lost a baby later on in pregnancy or had a stillbirth, surgery or other medical complication. Do discuss your history and health with your doctor or other trusted carer, who can help you decide when it is physically safe to begin trying again.

However, don't worry if you find yourself pregnant again before you have had the expected number of periods – relax, see your doctor and have a look at the guidelines further on in this chapter for taking good care of yourself in another pregnancy. Remember, every pregnancy is different and there is every chance of a good outcome next time around.

Your feelings

Only you know how you really feel about the prospect of another baby, and your feelings are likely to be very mixed, especially if you do become pregnant. There may be joy mixed with apprehension, continued grief for your other baby, fear of another loss, and guilt because you are now happy at the prospect of another baby. These emotions can be difficult to sort through on your own. Consider joining a support group for women who are experiencing pregnancy after loss, or seeing a therapist who specializes in grief support. You also need to find the right balance between remaining optimistic throughout another pregnancy and accepting the possibility of another loss.

Bear in mind that if you have experienced previous pregnancy or baby loss, you may be at increased risk of ante-natal depression, which some experts consider should be more actively diagnosed in order to help prevent its better-known component, post-natal depression. An estimated 50 per cent of women who experience depression during pregnancy also experience depression after the birth. A study reported in the *British Medical Journal* suggests that new mothers should be screened for the warning signs of depression long before delivery day. Many of the symptoms of ante-natal depression mimic common pregnancy complaints, such as fatigue, insomnia and appetite changes. But if those symptoms are accompanied by such classic depression symptoms as persistent sadness, a loss of enjoyment of life, anxiety, an inability to concentrate and/or extreme irritability, you should at least consider the possibility that you could be suffering from ante-natal depression, and ask your doctor, midwife or health visitor for advice accordingly.

Your relationship

As we've seen, losing a baby can have a dramatic impact on couples. This is a shared decision, so you may need to ask yourself whether your relationship has recovered and is strong enough for the challenge of another pregnancy.

Your situation

Now's the time to think about any external circumstances that could affect your decision. Can you foresee any other big life changes in the near future, such as moving house or changing jobs? What about any other children – how much attention do they need, and how close in age would you want your children to be?

A pre-conception health check-up

Before you start thinking of conceiving again you may find it helpful to see your doctor to check your reproductive and general health, and/or a geneticist who can advise you on any inherited conditions that may affect your baby. Your doctor can check for any general health conditions such as anaemia, and now is a chance to discuss any lifestyle or environmental factors that may impact on another pregnancy – e.g. a job that involves a lot of travel, driving or physical activity, or exposure to hazardous agents.

Your doctor can also check for immunity to both rubella (German measles) and chickenpox. Women do not always realize that, even if they have been vaccinated previously, immunity does not last for life. Before trying to conceive, ask your doctor for a blood test to check your immunity. If you are vaccinated against rubella, you will need to wait three months after the injection before getting pregnant.

If you or your partner take medication for a long-term condition, check with your consultant whether this may affect fertility or pregnancy outcome. It is generally best to avoid all medication unless you check with your GP first that it is safe to take while trying to conceive, or in early pregnancy.

Another point to consider is how you may feel, if you do become pregnant again, about ante-natal tests such as scans and amniocentesis. A test is useful when it identifies situations that can be monitored to prevent problems.

Extra support

Make sure that your doctor and midwife know your history and understand that you will need extra reassurance and perhaps extra scans and other ante-natal care. If you don't feel that your carers are as supportive as you'd like, consider finding a new doctor or midwife.

Where to give birth

Will the birth take place in the hospital where you lost your previous baby? Arrange one or more tours of the maternity unit. If you have strong feelings about wanting to give birth in a particular room or choosing a different birth room, put this in your birth plan. While it may not always be possible for the hospital to accommodate your wishes, it doesn't hurt to ask.

Repeated loss

Even if you have had several losses, you still have a good chance of a successful pregnancy, even if doctors were unable to discover the causes of the past pregnancy losses. However, you will need prompt and early care from your doctor in the event of another pregnancy.

You may also need extra emotional resilience as you face the question: 'Can I do this one more time?' It will help if you have, or can find, a person prepared to provide extra support for your pregnancy – a close friend or your doctor, perhaps even a private midwife.

Sadly, some women may also have to decide when to stop 'trying again', for medical or emotional reasons – whether on a temporary or permanent basis. They may no longer be able to take the profound stress of another pregnancy and loss, or in a few rare cases may even be medically advised against it. Deciding to stop in itself creates another loss, which may mean mourning again all the previous losses, and the loss of the life and the children that will never be.

While this goes beyond the scope of this book, it is important to stress again the importance of getting support, and if necessary professional counselling, for yourself and your partner.

Fertility

Another point to bear in mind is that deciding to 'try' does not automatically guarantee a pregnancy. It can be a shock for couples to find that another pregnancy doesn't happen immediately. However, there is in fact only a 20 per cent chance of conceiving at any time, so if it doesn't happen at once, don't worry. Again, relax, get some exercise, don't drink or smoke, and look at the guidelines further on in this chapter for healthy diet.

Having a miscarriage doesn't mean per se that you have a fertility problem, and the vast majority of women go on to have healthy pregnancies. Even after repeated miscarriages (three or more in a row) you still have a 70–80 per cent chance of carrying another pregnancy to term.

Unfortunately, if you had a pregnancy loss due to ectopic pregnancy, there is a 20 per cent risk that a further pregnancy could become ectopic, and this may affect your fertility. This may be something you want to discuss with your doctor.

Boost your chances of conceiving:

- Take regular exercise.
- Eat a healthy diet, with organic food if possible as pesticides affect your oestrogen levels. Cut out anything with additives and preservatives.
- Try to keep your weight within reasonable limits.
- Reduce or cut out alcohol.
- Reduce or cut out coffee and other caffeine-rich drinks.
- Stop smoking.
- Start taking folic acid (see p. 84).
- Don't take any unnecessary medication.
- Relax! Stress is known to release certain chemicals in the brain that can interfere with the production of your normal pregnancy hormones.
- Don't plan sex. Sperm survives more during spontaneous, enjoyable sex than in planned baby-making sex.
- Suggest your partner wears boxers, not briefs. The testicles benefit from not being constricted.

Genetic counselling

Genetic counselling is specialized medical advice on a person's or couple's individual chance of inherited disease and how this may affect the outcome of a pregnancy. If you know there is genetic disease in the family, it would be wise to consider this. You might also want to discuss genetic counselling with your doctor if any of your pregnancies were known to be affected by genetic factors, or if you have had recurrent miscarriages.

The counsellor can help you make a record of your family medical history and your own medical background, and may arrange blood tests or other tests to help assess your individual chance of having a child affected by a certain genetic condition.

A genetic counsellor can advise on how likely a problem may be to recur, along with information about any available tests.

Taking care of your next pregnancy

Research from the Miscarriage Association shows that nearly half of the women who had experienced loss in pregnancy did not feel well informed about what was happening to them, and only 29 per cent felt well cared for emotionally. Information is a vital part of coping with the experience of loss – it also helps you minimize the risk of anything happening to your next pregnancy.

The latest research suggests the following guidelines for a best healthy pregnancy outcome:

Avoid passive smoking

A Harvard School of Public Health study found that a third of women whose partners smoked more than 20 cigarettes a day lost their babies within six weeks of conceiving. For women with non-smoking partners, the rate was 20 per cent. The toxins in cigarettes affect the chromosomes, or genetic information, on your partner's sperm. Second-hand smoke also damages your growing baby by reducing blood flow through the placenta.

Deal with fibroids

If you know you have fibroids (something which often shows up in a previous pregnancy) ask your doctor if these can be dealt with before conceiving again. Women with smaller uterine fibroids, not larger ones, have a greater chance of miscarriage, say scientists at the

University of North Carolina. Fibroids are benign muscle tumours that affect 20 per cent of women of reproductive age.

Have any infections treated

Certain infections, such as toxoplasmosis, can threaten a pregnancy or the health of your baby. It may be advisable to avoid contact with raw meat, soil, cat litter and farm animals, especially during lambing, in early pregnancy. If you suspect that you or your partner might have a sexually transmitted infection, both of you should check this before trying to conceive, via your GP or a confidential genito-urinary medicine clinic. A study at St George's Hospital in London found that women who were treated with antibiotics for bacterial vaginosis had 10 per cent fewer miscarriages than those given a placebo.

If you have a long-term condition such as diabetes, high blood pressure, epilepsy or PCOS (polycystic ovary syndrome), ask your doctor for advice on your best chances of becoming pregnant and any extra care that may be needed.

Avoid the Atkins diet

Results of a study at the Colorado Center for Reproductive Medicine showed that mice on high-protein diets were 20 per cent less likely to have a full-term pregnancy. Over three million people in the UK currently follow the controversial diet. Its emphasis on meat can overload your body with protein, hindering your baby's development and doubling the risk of genetic problems. The advice is to forget Atkins if you're trying to conceive.

Enjoy a massage

Joint research from the March of Dimes and the Johnson & Johnson Pediatric Institute in the USA showed that full body massage from a woman's partner can lower the risk of miscarriage – it reduces her stress hormones and can lead to more full-term births. These results are supported by an earlier study from the University of California.

Drink coffee in moderation

The *British Medical Journal* reports that women who drink more than eight cups of coffee a day triple their risk of having a stillbirth, and four to seven cups increase the risk by 80 per cent.

Just don't smoke

Apart from its harmful effects during pregnancy, smoking increases the chances of cot death. If you smoke while pregnant (as 30 per cent of female smokers do), then your baby is more likely to die from SIDS (Sudden Infant Death Syndrome), according to US researchers. They found that smoking during pregnancy can damage key receptors in the brain which control breathing, and that this damage could cause your baby to stop breathing after they're born, for no apparent reason.

Buy a new mattress for your baby

Doctors from the Royal Hospital for Sick Children in Glasgow found that if a mattress had been handed down to a mother from another home, the baby faced a significantly higher risk of dying from SIDS, potentially because of toxic bacteria present. However, despite the proven link between toxic bacteria and cot death, the Foundation for the Study of Infant Deaths (FSID) said what mattered was that your baby's mattress was clean, firm and well-fitting, preferably with a complete PVC or removable washable cover.

Keep it cool

An FSID study showed that many parents unwittingly keep their baby's room too warm. One in five thought that it should be hotter than the recommended range of 16–20°C, and only one in three had a thermometer in their baby's room.

Think carefully about bed-sharing

It's cosy, easier for feeding and enables you to get more sleep, and some parents also feel reassured by having their baby next to them in bed, so they can check their child's breathing and general comfort. However, letting your baby sleep with you, especially when eight weeks or younger, increases the risk of cot death, according to research from FSID, which recommends your baby sleeps in a cot in your bedroom for the first six months. You certainly should not share a bed with your baby if you or your partner smoke, have been drinking alcohol, take medication that makes you sleepy, or feel very tired.

Nutrition in pregnancy

This time round you may be looking for foolproof ways to safeguard your pregnancy, and one of these may well be your diet. Obviously, eating well will give your baby the best start in life, but try not to become too anxious about what you do and don't eat, as diet in itself is highly unlikely to threaten the health of your baby. However, you yourself will probably feel better and more relaxed if you do eat as well as possible.

Start taking folic acid

This is perhaps the most important dietary step you can take to help protect your growing baby's health, especially before conception and during the first trimester of pregnancy. Up to 70 per cent of all neural tube defects, such as spina bifida, could be prevented if pregnant women ate or took a daily folic acid supplement.

From the moment you start trying to conceive until around the end of the first three months, aim to take a daily 400mcg supplement of folic acid. Women with a history of neural tube defects should be prescribed a 5mg supplement, so do consult your doctor about supplements you might need.

As well as supplements, eat foods rich in folic acid such as green leafy vegetables (cabbage, broccoli, spinach, Brussels sprouts, spring greens, kale, okra and fresh peas); fortified breakfast cereals; wholemeal and wholegrain breads and rolls; pulses such as chickpeas, black-eyed beans and lentils.

Folic acid is easily lost during cooking, so steam vegetables or cook in only a little water for a short time to retain as much goodness as possible.

Eat foods rich in iron

Iron is necessary to make haemoglobin, which carries oxygen in blood cells.

Iron-rich foods include meat-based sources, such as lean red meat, and plant-based sources, such as fortified breakfast cereals, eggs, baked beans and other pulses, green leafy vegetables such as spinach and broccoli, dried apricots and prunes, wholegrain breads and cereals. Your body doesn't absorb iron from non-meat foods as easily as it does from meat sources, but you can help the process by including a source of vitamin C with your meal, such as fresh berries or citrus fruit, or a glass of orange juice. Good sources of vitamin C include citrus fruits (oranges, tangerines, grapefruit and lemons), blackcurrants, strawberries, kiwi fruit, peppers, tomatoes and green leafy vegetables. Your iron levels will be checked throughout pregnancy, and if necessary you'll be prescribed a supplement. Consult your doctor about supplements you might need.

Avoid caffeine

Drinking more than four cups of coffee a day has been linked to an increase risk of miscarriage, stillbirths and low birth weight. Caffeine also inhibits the absorption of iron from your food. Instead, try decaffeinated tea and coffee, herbal teas or green tea.

You don't have to eat for two!

During pregnancy, your body becomes more efficient at absorbing nutrients in the digestive system, and also stores vitamins and minerals rather than excreting them. Aim to eat better, not more. You only need an extra 200–300 calories per day in your *final* trimester, for a total of 2,500 calories (200 calories can be a Marmite sandwich and glass of low-fat milk). If you have morning sickness you may not feel like eating, but during the second and third trimesters your appetite will increase. Your weight gain should be between 15 and 35 pounds. Eat smaller meals every three to four hours.

Plan your shopping

Food consumption starts with purchase, so plan what you will buy before going out. Good items to put on your list include fresh fruit and vegetables, wholemeal pasta, brown rice and potatoes, turkey and chicken.

Increase your fibre intake

Fibre helps you to avoid constipation and piles. Eat fruit and vegetables, wholemeal bread and cereals, brown rice, wholemeal pasta and pulses, and make sure you are drinking enough.

Eat carbohydrates at every meal

Carbohydrates are good because they give you vital energy and fuel the growth of your baby, as well as providing B vitamins, essential for a healthy nervous system. They should make up one-third of your daily calorie intake.

Ensure you have enough calcium

You need an extra 40 per cent of calcium a day to ensure your baby's bones and teeth develop properly. This is equivalent to an extra three cups of milk a day.

Good sources include milk and dairy foods such as cheese, yoghurt and fromage frais; bread; green vegetables; canned fish with soft, edible bones (salmon, sardines and pilchards); dried apricots; sesame seeds; tofu; fortified orange juice; and fortified soya milk.

Vitamin D is required for the body to use calcium. Natural sunlight, in moderation, is the perfect source, but given our climate you may well be lacking in it! Also, if you don't drink milk or eat eggs or oily fish, ask your GP about taking a vitamin D supplement.

Avoid soft cheeses, raw seafood and unpasteurized milk

All are sources of bacteria, listeriosis and toxoplasmosis, which can cause miscarriage and stillbirths. But omega-3, found in oily fish, is still vital for the brain's development, so grilled salmon or mackerel is OK. A recent Danish study showed that eating two portions of oily fish a week could help reduce the chance of a premature birth and a low birth weight.

Be careful with liver and pâté

Although they are good sources of iron, they also contain high concentrations of vitamin A, which can build up in your liver and harm your baby. But don't avoid fruit and vegetable sources of vitamin A, aka carotene – they're fine.

Help your partner's fertility

Did you know that zinc, selenium and magnesium are essential for healthy sperm? Make sure your partner is getting enough by eating lots of mushrooms, eggs, tuna, broccoli and beans.

When you do become pregnant

Most women become pregnant within the year following the loss of their baby. While it is a joyful day when you get that positive result, once you do get pregnant again it may be hard to keep your worries at bay. While you're probably better informed and more aware than you were before, you know you are still powerless over the eventual outcome. There are steps you can take to handle this anxiety, however.

Ask for extra support and reassurance

When you go to your GP to confirm your pregnancy, explain how anxious you are. To put your mind at ease, most GPs will arrange for more regular screening.

After her ectopic pregnancy, Tina had early scans in her next pregnancy to make sure the baby was in the right place. When Sarah became pregnant again after her first miscarriage, her midwife was very good and sent her for a scan at seven weeks, even though she had received a letter from the hospital saying, 'Please do not send worried patients for scans.' They claimed it was wasting their time! Sarah was reassured from the moment she saw the heartbeat.

Lorraine
When I finally became pregnant again, I was beside myself the whole time. I must have been a nightmare. I had three bleeding episodes, so each time I presumed I had miscarried the baby, but after each scan he was still there, heart beating away. When I got further on, I convinced myself my baby would be stillborn – after all, I'd had miscarriages and an ectopic pregnancy, so why not a stillbirth? My carers were excellent and arranged daily monitoring for me. Without that, I would have gone mad, and that isn't an exaggeration!

You can also buy or rent your own foetal heartbeat monitor, so you can listen whenever you have the urge. These are very reassuring, but they're not completely foolproof, so don't rely on them alone.

Sarah
I didn't buy anything for a long time, but I did buy a Doppler machine which was the *best* thing I ever purchased. I would recommend any mother who is worried to buy or rent one of these as you can pick up your baby's heartbeat really early. I was only nine weeks and four days pregnant when I first heard my son's heartbeat, and just a quick listen would reassure me for the rest of the day.

Monitoring during the birth is also important. Given your history, this will probably be provided, but do also arrange for a strong supportive birth partner to speak up for you to staff.

Sarah
When I finally gave birth, I was ecstatic! The hospital staff were excellent; I was monitored throughout my labour. When they handed him to me – I can't begin to describe the relief I felt at my

baby being born well and beautiful. I also felt really stupid for worrying that something might have been wrong in the first place!

Take a short-term view

Make your motto: 'Just get through today, don't worry about tomorrow.' It can be hard to see how you're going to make it mentally through the next nine months because it seems such a long time away. Rather than looking at it as such a big chunk of time, break it down into smaller, more manageable bite-size amounts, as you would any big work task. Really do focus on one day at a time, because as each day passes uneventfully you will gain more confidence in yourself and your body, and start to relax more and enjoy yourself, starting a positive-thinking cycle. Remember, there is rarely anything that is as threatening as the imagination.

Live a little

Try to relax and continue with your usual enjoyable activities. Do things that will take your mind off your anxieties. Don't overdo things. You need to make this pregnancy as stress-free as possible. Incorporate as many enjoyable things into your routine as you can. Watch a good comedy and listen to your favourite music. Make the most of your time with your partner before your baby arrives. Don't focus all your conversations on your baby, otherwise your relationship will become very one-dimensional. Think back to what you both liked to do when you were dating or before you had kids, and do these things again.

Getting past milestones

For some women, every day can be a milestone and pregnancy takes a long, long time. For others, there will be specific flashpoints during the pregnancy – the day the bleeding started, the date of the scan which showed no heartbeat.

Sarah

What helped me get past my 'danger' point of 12 weeks was speaking to my partner, family and friends. They were very positive and spoke about 'the baby arriving' when all I could say was 'if the baby arrives'. Listening to such positive thinking does help. I also focused on getting to the next day and adding another day to the amount of time I'd been pregnant.

Kate

Every day and every week was a milestone. I had to try and stay positive and not constantly think, 'Oh my God, we have *x* weeks to go,' rather than, 'Wow, we have made it through *x* weeks with no problems.'

Try and plan a scan for milestones and talk to your partner, friends and family when that day looms. There is no magic cure for getting through this day, but once it's over a big weight will be lifted from your shoulders. Do also plan for being late – most pregnancies continue past their due date. Mentally add on another ten days, and arrange to see friends and keep gently occupied during this time.

Don't be afraid to bond with your baby in case something goes wrong again. The chances are it won't. Probably the worst hurdle you'll have to get through is the danger point from your last pregnancy.

Tina

I was still worried but I made a real effort to think about the baby and imagine him arriving. I would visualize things to do with the baby, such as the birth, being in hospital, and coming home.

When I had my first live birth, with my son Malachi, I was induced before having an emergency C-section. He was kept with me until I woke up. My partner showed him to me and I kissed him before he was taken away to special care. When I saw him the next morning, I thought, 'Where did he come from?' I fell in love with him immediately and I knew the pain I'd been through with my two recent miscarriages had been worth it. I would have gone through a hundred pregnancies just to be his mum.

My losses have made me realize how lucky I am to have my children. People are shocked when I say I've been pregnant ten times and lost seven children. I think maybe I'm not tough enough on my children. I'm also aware of the fact that I could lose them at any time. I want every part of their lives to be happy. I want them to experience as much of life as they can and to share these experiences with them because time goes by so quickly.

Never give up trying, because the minute you see your healthy child, it's worth it.

Kate

With my subsequent pregnancies after my two miscarriages and three stillbirths (one set of twins), I bought my own foetal heart monitor and did very frequent scans. After my first miscarriage, it was really hard not to worry as I didn't have any other children to come home to, but after the twins died it wasn't as bad because I had my three-year-old, Henry.

When I had Henry, I was absolutely ecstatic. I had my C-section in the evening and I was so happy to have a live baby I was up bathing him the next morning. With Ollie, my second live birth, it was horrible because he caught a cold and had to go to the special care unit, which needn't have happened if I'd been assertive and made them put him skin to skin.

When I gave birth to Robert in December 2003, it was absolutely fantastic as I was discharged the very same day and had my family home in time for Christmas.

My losses have put life into a different perspective. Nothing is as important as my children. I have a few philosophies on life:

- If you take it, you will get it, good or bad.
- I would not change my life for anyone else's. Although we've been through hell, my family are all that matter for me.
- What is the worst thing that could happen? If you are prepared for the worst, anything better will be wonderful.
- I'm positive, but prepared.

As a parent, don't blindly trust doctors and nurses. Always question anything you don't understand. We're all too concerned about what others think about us and not upsetting our midpartner. Demand to see the consultant if you're concerned. It's their job. Learn as much as you can about pregnancy and birth, and trust your instincts and your body.

Your ten-point worry control checklist

Don't worry about worrying

Tina

As for the fear of miscarrying again, well, that is always there. It's OK to worry. I know it might sound stupid, but I always instinctively knew if I was going to miscarry or if I was going to be all right. After your friends get sick about hearing baby talk, an online support group is great because everyone is in the same boat and nothing sounds like a silly question.

Write down your worries, so you don't get carried away

What is the cause of your worry and why does it worry you? Include all the possible solutions that are available to you and the pros and cons of each, followed by the best option. Most importantly, what is the first thing you can do as part of that solution that will have the most positive impact in solving your worry?

Distinguish between big and little worries

Determining the importance of your worry is a very personal matter. Once you've written down your worries, give them a rating out of ten for impact and likelihood of happening. The ones with the lowest ranking are relatively small worries.

A worry shared is a worry halved

Don't try and cope on your own if you're feeling swamped and not sure of the best way to solve your worries. Sharing them with a close friend or even someone removed from the situation can give you a different perspective and make you realize that things aren't as bad as they seem.

Ask yourself, 'What really is the worst that could happen?' and be realistic

The chances that you will lose your baby again are slim. Use the law of averages to control your fears, and get the facts so you can disprove your worry when you sit down and think about it logically. By playing devil's advocate, ask what are the odds that the worst-case scenario will happen. Now write down what you would do if it did happen, then forget about it, secure in the knowledge that you could cope if it did come true. Psychologists say that compulsive worriers endlessly try to rehearse for things that might go wrong and don't balance this with expectations or readiness for good outcomes. They can't let go and have life work for them. Imagine your worry is your best friend's. How would you advise them?

Visualize a positive resolution

Use this favoured technique of counsellors – picture in your mind the feeling you will have when you positively resolve a worry. Even if you're not yet sure how you're going to resolve it, create images of how much more secure you will feel having worked it through. This will give you the subconscious stimulus to go on and find the solution.

Have the wisdom to let go of the uncontrollable

Realize that certain things are beyond your control, so try to allow some flexibility in your life. If you fixate on or worry about a particular outcome, then you're setting yourself up for disappointment if things don't go the way you wanted. Worrying about uncontrollable events is like trying to look into a crystal ball and predict with certainty what will happen.

What is your circle of influence?

If you can change or affect your worry then that's great, but be constructive and work on the problem. If you can't directly influence something that is worrying you, then try to find a small way in which you can make a difference.

Trust yourself and develop self-awareness

Worrying often stems from your lack of faith in yourself to deal with what's going on in your life, so building your confidence and self-esteem is important. You are powerful, not powerless. Make it your mission to learn why you ever thought you were powerless.

Develop a 'peace of mind' by learning to meditate

Sit down for a few minutes and focus on the sensation of your breath coming in and out of your nose. It feels a bit cooling when it comes in and warming when it goes out. Focus on that sensation for 15 minutes twice a day.

Conclusion

Moving on into a new future does not mean forgetting your baby. As Michelle says, while time does ease the pain you never stop grieving for the loss of a baby, and over the months and years grief can become a bitter-sweet bond with your lost child. There will always be reminders, such as seeing children the age your own child would have been had he or she lived.

The thought of moving on and looking to the future may initially seem disloyal to the memory of your baby. Some women may feel that letting go of their heartache means letting go of their last link with their baby. There may also be fear of the future: what if it happens again? Will I be strong enough for what life throws at me?

Unless you come to terms with your grief, frustration may build up and resurface months or even years later when your family and friends least expect it. However, your own urge to live and to move on also has to be respected. The important thing is that you recover in your own time, without feeling rushed by other people or yourself. Grief can be a natural healing process if it is lived through at its own pace.

Recovery is a gradual process, so don't expect too much too soon or set yourself impossibly high standards that you feel must be achieved. Finding joy in your life again, in any small way, means your journey to recovery has begun. You will learn some difficult and important lessons on the way, which will change you as a person. But the best way to honour the memory of your baby is to make the most of your life. Your choices and actions are a tribute to the baby or babies you have lost.

Useful Addresses

Helpful contacts

Action on Pre-eclampsia

84–88 Pinner Road
Harrow
Middlesex HA1 4HZ
Tel: 020 8427 4217
Website: www.apec.org.uk
Email: enquiries@apec.org.uk
Promotes medical research and educates about pre-eclampsia and supports sufferers and their families.

Antenatal Results and Choices (ARC)

73 Charlotte Street
London W1P 4PN
Tel: 020 7631 0280
Website: www.arc-uk.org
Email: arcsafa@aol.com
Helps parents who may have to make difficult decisions as a result of ante-natal testing.

The Association of Reflexologists

27 Old Gloucester Street
London WC1N 3XX
Tel: 0870 567 3320
Website: www.aor.org.uk
Email: info@aor.org.uk
Certifying body for reflexologists in the UK.

Bliss

68 South Lambeth Road
London SW8 1RL
Helpline: 0500 618 140
Tel: 020 7820 9471
Website: www.bliss.org.uk
Email: information@bliss.org.uk

Neonatal services and support to help more high-risk babies to survive.

The British Alliance of Healing Organisations

23 Nutcroft Grove
Fetcham
Leatherhead
Surrey KT22 9LA
Tel: 01372 373 241

British Association for Counselling and Psychotherapy

BACP House
35–37 Albert Street
Rugby CV21 2SG
Tel: 0870 443 5252
Website: www.bacp.co.uk
Email: bacp@bacp.co.uk
Disseminates counselling and psychotherapy information to the public.

British Complementary Medicine Association

PO Box 5122
Bournemouth BH8 0WG
Tel: 0845 345 5977
Website: www.bcma.co.uk
Email: info@bcma.co.uk
Supports delivery of high-quality complementary medicine to the public.

British Homeopathic Association

Hahnemann House
29 Park Street West
Luton LU1 3BE
Tel: 0870 444 3950
Website: www.trusthomeopathy.org
Email: via web page

British Organ Donor Society (BODY)

Balsham
Cambridge CB1 6DL
Tel: 01223 893 636
Website: www.argonet.co.uk/body/

Email: body@argonet.co.uk
Covers topics on organ donation and transplantation, both in the UK and worldwide.

British Wheel of Yoga

25 Jermyn Street
Sleaford
Lincolnshire NG34 7RU
Tel: 01529 306 851
Website: www.bwy.org.uk
Email: information@bwy.org.uk

The Child Bereavement Trust

Aston House
West Wycombe
High Wycombe
Buckinghamshire HP14 3AG
Tel: 0845 357 1000
Website: www.childbereavement.org.uk
Email: enquiries@childbereavement.org.uk
Centre of excellence for improving the care offered by professionals to grieving families.

The Child Death Helpline

The Bereavement Services Department
Great Ormond Street Hospital
Great Ormond Street
London WC1N 3JH
Tel: 0800 282 986
Website: www.childdeathhelpline.org.uk
Professionals and parents provide a listening service that offers emotional support to all those affected by the death of a child.

Chinese Medical Institute and Register (UK)

103–105 Camden High Street
London NW1 7JN
Tel: 020 7388 6704

The Compassionate Friends

53 North Street
Bristol BS3 1EN
Helpline: 08451 232 304

Tel: 08451 203 785
Website: www.tcf.org.uk
Email: information@tcf.org.uk
Bereaved parents who support and assist other families towards positive resolution of grief after the death of a child of any age.

Cot Death Society

4 West Mills Yard
Kennet Road
Newbury
Berkshire RG14 5LP
Tel: 0845 601 0234
Website: www.cotdeathsociety.org.uk
Email: fundraising@cotdeathsociety.org.uk
Provides advice on how to avoid cot death and provides, on medical referral, infant respiration monitors for UK families who have a baby at risk from cot death.

Cruse Bereavement Care

Cruse House
126 Sheen Road
Richmond
Surrey TW9 1UR
Helpline: 0870 167 1677
Website: www.crusebereavementcare.org.uk
Email: helpline@crusebereavementcare.org.uk
A charity providing free advice to anyone affected by a bereavement, as well as support and counselling.

Depression Alliance Perinatal Depression Helpline (DAPeND)

Tel: 020 8768 0123 (7 p.m.–10 p.m. weekdays)
Helpline providing support for mothers and pregnant women who are isolated and lonely or experiencing post-natal illness.

FSID (Foundation for the Study of Infant Deaths)

Artillery House
11–19 Artillery Row
London SW1P 1RT
Helpline: 0870 787 0554
Tel: 0870 787 0885
Website: www.sids.org.uk

Email: fsid@sids.org.uk
Support for bereaved families and advice on how to reduce the risk of cot death.

Healer Foundation

Sunday School House
The Village
Thurstonland
Huddersfield
West Yorkshire HD4 6XX
Tel: 01924 386860
Website: www.healerfound.co.uk
Email: info@healerfound.co.uk

International Federation of Aromatherapists

IFA
182 Chiswick High Road
London W4 1PP
Tel: 020 8742 2605
Website: www.ifaroma.org
Email: office@ifaroma.org

The International Federation of Professional Aromatherapists

82 Ashby Road
Hinckley
Leicestershire LE10 1SN
Tel: 01455 637 987
Website: www.ifparoma.org
Email: admin@IFPAroma.org
Largest professional aromatherapy practitioner organization in the world. Promotes educational standards among aromatherapists.

International Star Registry

23–28 Penn Street
London N1 5DL
Tel: 020 7684 4444
Website: www.international-star-registry.org

Jewish Bereavement Counselling Service

8/10 Forty Avenue
Wembley
Middlesex HA9 8JW

Tel: 020 8385 1874
Website: www.jvisit.org.uk/jbcs
Email: jbcs@jvisit.org.uk
A team of volunteer bereavement counsellors helping members of
the Jewish community.

London Bereavement Network

c/o 61 Philpot Street
London E1 2JH
Tel: 020 7247 1209
Website: www.bereavement.org.uk
Email: info@bereavement.org.uk
Provides information and support to members of the public who are
bereaved and the professionals who support them.

MIND

Granta House
15–19 Broadway
Stratford
London E15 4BQ
Helpline: 0845 766 0163
Website: www.mind.org.uk
Email: contact@mind.org.uk
Helps anyone experiencing mental distress.

The Miscarriage Association

c/o Clayton Hospital
Northgate
Wakefield
West Yorkshire WF1 3JS
Tel: 01924 200 799
Website: www.miscarriageassociation.org.uk
Email: info@miscarriageassociation.org.uk
Support and information for those suffering the effects of pregnancy
loss.

National Association of Bereavement Services (NABS)

2nd Floor
4 Pinchin Street
London E1 6DB
Tel: 020 7709 9090

Has a national directory of bereavement and loss services, and can direct people to their nearest appropriate source of support.

National Institute of Medical Herbalists

Elm House
54 Mary Arches Street
Exeter EX4 3BA
Tel: 01392 426 022
Website: www.nimh.org.uk
Email: nimh@ukexeter.freeserve.co.uk
Research and practice of herbal medicine by trained and accredited members.

The National Memorial Arboretum

Croxall Road
Alrewas
Burton-upon-Trent DE13 7AR
Tel: 01283 792 333
Website: www.nationalmemorialarboretum.co.uk
Email: nmarboretum@btconnect.com
Within this 150-acre arboretum is a garden for lost children. Trees can be planted in a child's name.

Penhaligon's Friends

PO Box 11
Camborne
Cornwall TR1 8YG
Tel: 0845 607 1943
Website: www.penhaligonsfriends.org.uk
Email: editor@penhaligonsfriends.org.uk
Support group for bereaved children and their families in Cornwall.

Professional Guild of NLP

PO Box 104
Clitheroe
Lancashire BB7 9ZG
Tel: 0845 226 7334
Website: www.professionalguildofnlp.com
Email: info@professionalguildofnlp.com

Relate

Website: www.relate.org.uk
Email: enquiries@relate.org.uk
Provides confidential relationship counselling and support services.
Local centres are listed in the phone book.

The Samaritans

Tel: 08457 90 90 90
Website: www.samaritans.org.uk
Email: jo@samaritans.org
Provides confidential 24-hour emotional support for people feeling
distress or despair.

SANDS (Stillbirth and Neonatal Death Society)

28 Portland Place
London W1N 1LY
Helpline: 020 7436 5881
Website: www.uk-sands.org
Email: support@uk-sands.org
Support for parents and families whose baby is stillborn or dies soon
after birth.

Scottish Cot Death Trust

Royal Hospital for Sick Children
Yorkhill
Glasgow G3 8SJ
Tel: 0141 357 3946
Website: www.sidscotland.org.uk
Email: contact@sidscotland.org.uk
Researches the possible causes of cot death and supports families
affected by it.

SIBBS (Support in Bereavement for Brothers and Sisters)

PO Box 1246
Bristol BS99 2UH
Tel: 0117 966 5202
Website: www.tcf.org.uk
Email: sibs@tcf.org.uk
Support group for siblings within The Compassionate Friends.

Tommy's

Tommy's Head Office
Nicholas House
3 Laurence Pountney Hill
London EC4R 0BB
Tel: 0870 777 3060
Website: www.tommys-campaign.org
Email: info@tommys.org
Research, education and information to help prevent premature birth, miscarriage and stillbirth.

Twins and Multiple Births Association (TAMBA)

The Willows
Gardner Road
Guildford
Surrey GU1 4PG
Tel: 0870 770 3305
Web: www.tamba.org.uk
Offers bereavement support specific to twins and multiples.

UK Reiki Federation

PO Box 1785
Andover SP11 0WB
Tel: 01264 773 774
Website: www.reikifed.co.uk
Email: enquiry@reikifed.co.uk

Yorkhill Family Bereavement Service

Yorkhill NHS Trust
Yorkhill
Glasgow G3 8SJ
Tel: 0141 201 9257
Website: www.2-in-2-1.co.uk/services/yorkhill
Email: terri.winkler@yorkhill.scot.nhs.uk
Provides support to people affected by the death of a child.

Useful websites

Grief and Loss Resource Centre

Website: www.rockies.net/~spirit/grief/grief.html
Email: cef@rockies.net

Pregnancy Loss

Website: www.pregnancyloss.info
Email: www.pregnancyloss.info/guestbook.html

UK Funerals On-line

Website: www.uk-funerals.co.uk
Email: info@uk-funerals.co.uk

Organizations outside the UK

American Pregnancy Association

1425 Greenway Drive
Suite 440
Irving
Texas 75038
USA
Tel (in USA): 1 800 672 2296
Website: www.americanpregnancy.org
Email: Questions@AmericanPregnancy.org
Committed to resolving reproductive, pregnancy and sexual health concerns through education, research, advocacy and community awareness.

American Society for Reproductive Medicine

1209 Montgomery Highway
Birmingham
Alabama 35216-2809
USA
Tel: (+1) 205 978 5000
Website: www.asrm.org
Email: asrm@asrm.org and asrm@asrm-dc.org
Promotes advancement of the art, science and practice of reproductive medicine through education and research, and through advocacy on behalf of patients, physicians and affiliated healthcare providers.

American Sudden Infant Death Syndrome (SIDS) Institute

509 Augusta Drive
Marietta
Georgia 30067
USA

Tel: (+1) 770 426 8746 or (in USA) 800 232-SIDS
Website: www.sids.org/
Email: www.sids.org/online
Dedicated to preventing sudden infant death and to promoting infant health through research, clinical services, education and family support.

Bonnie Babes Foundation

Victoria (Head Office)
PO Box 2220
Rowville
VIC 3152
Australia
Tel: (+03) 9758 2800
Website: www.bbf.org.au/home.asp
Email: enquiry@bbf.org.au

Center for Loss in Multiple Birth (CLIMB)

c/o Jean Kollantai
PO Box 91377
Anchorage
AK 99509
USA
Tel: (+1) 907 222 5321/274 7029 (Lisa Fleischer)
Website: climb-support.org/index.html
Email: climb@pobox.alaska.net
Provides parent-to-parent support for parents who have lost one or more multiple birth children from conception through birth, infancy and early childhood.

The Compassionate Friends

PO Box 3696
Oak Brook
IL 60522-3696
USA
Tel: (+1) 630 990 0010 or (in USA) 877 969 0010
Website: www.compassionatefriends.org
Email: nationaloffice@compassionatefriends.org
Offers friendship and understanding to bereaved parents primarily through local chapters.

Foundation for Blood Research

PO Box 190
8 Nonesuch Road
Scarborough
ME 04070-0190
USA
Tel: (+1) 207 883 4131
Website: www.fbr.org
Email: www.fbr.org/contact-form.html
Aims to find better ways to identify, manage and prevent disease through scientific investigation, outreach science education, public health programme design, population screening and clinical testing.

HAND (Helping After Neonatal Death)

PO Box 341
Los Gatos
CA 95031
USA
Tel: 1 888 908-HAND or 1 408 995 6102
Website: www.handonline.org
Email: info@handonline.org
A Californian non-profit organization helping parents, their families and their healthcare providers cope with the loss of a baby before, during or after birth.

The Hannah's Heart Network

15105-D John J. Delaney Blvd
Charlotte
NC 28277
USA
Tel: (+1) 704 541 5091
Website: www.hannahsheartnetwork.org
Email: amanda@hannahsheartnetwork.org
A network of women who believe children are a gift from God and who have experienced or are experiencing infertility, miscarriage, early infant death, secondary infertility, assisted reproductive technology procedures and adoption.

HOPE (Helping Other Parents Endure)

Tel: (+1) 770 424 8326
Various regional agencies in the USA.

HopeXchange

26 Towne Centre Way #731
Hampton
Virginia 23666
USA
Tel: (+1) 757 826 2162
Website: www.hopexchange.com
Email: info@HopeXchange.com
Company offering support to those coping with miscarriage, stillbirth or infant death.

HOPING (Helping Other Parents in Normal Grieving)

Sparrow Hospital
1215 E. Michigan Ave
PO Box 30480
Lansing
MI 48090-9986
USA
Tel: (+1) 517 484 3873

Hygeia Foundation

Website: www.hygeia.com
Email: judelsondr@ajdj.com
Provides information on many different areas of women's health and links to related websites.

The Irish Sudden Infant Death Association

Carmichael House
4 North Brunswick Street
Dublin 7
Helpline in Ireland: 1850 391 391
Tel: (+353) 1873 2711
Website: www.iol.ie/~isidansr
Email: kibnsidr@iol.ie

The March of Dimes

1275 Mamaroneck Avenue
White Plains
NY 10605
USA

Website: www.marchofdimes.com
Email: www.marchofdimes.com/aboutus
Aims to improve the health of babies by preventing birth defects and infant mortality, through research, community services, education and advocacy to save babies' lives.

Miscarriage, Infant Death and Stillbirth (MIDS)

16 Crescent Drive
Parsippany
NY 07054
USA

Miscarriage Support Auckland

PO Box 14
7011 Ponsonby
Auckland
New Zealand
Tel: (+64) 09 378 4060
Website: www.miscarriagesupport.org.nz
Email: support@miscarriagesupport.org.nz
A team of volunteers who have all experienced infant loss and give others emotional support.

Mothers In Sympathy and Support (MISS)

PO Box 5333
Peoria
Arizona 85385-5333
USA
Tel: (+1) 623 979 1000
Website: www.missfoundation.org
Email: info@missfoundation.org
Online support site for family members experiencing the death of a child.

The National Partnership to Help Pregnant Smokers Quit

725 Airport Road
CB # 7590
Chapel Hill
NC 27599-7590
USA
Tel: (+1) 919 843 7663

Website: www.helppregnantsmokersquit.org
Email: info@helppregantsmokersquit.org
A coalition of American organizations aimed at increasing the number of pregnant women who quit smoking. It wants to ensure all pregnant women in the United States are screened for tobacco use, and receive best-practice cessation counselling as part of prenatal care.

Pain, Heartache and Hope

2710 Knoxville Drive
League City
Texas 77573
USA
Website: www.pain-heartache-hope.com
Email: through website
Support group for men and women coping with infertility, miscarriage, stillbirth and the loss of a child.

Pregnancy and Infant Loss Center

1421 East Wayzata Blvd #70
Wayzata
MN 55391
USA
Tel: (+1) 612 473 9372
Website:
www.bloomington.in.us/socserv/mit/PREGNANCY_AND_
INFANT_LOSS_CENTER.html
Offers support, resources and education on miscarriage, stillbirth and newborn death.

Premature

Suite 100
10200 Old Katy Road
Houston
TX 77043
USA
Bereavement support group.

Premature and High Risk Infant Association

PO Box 37114
Peoria
IL 61614

USA
Provides information on premature babies.

Resolve Through Sharing (RTS)

Many local chapters in the USA.
Supports those who have lost a baby through miscarriage, stillbirth or newborn death.

SHARE

St Joseph Health Center
300 First Capitol Drive
St Charles
MO 63301-2893
USA
Tel: (in USA) 1 800 821 6819 or (+1) 636 947 6164
Website: www.NationalSHAREOffice.com
Email: share@nationalshareoffice.com
Supports those affected by early pregnancy loss, stillbirth or newborn death.

Shattered Dreams (Miscarriage)

21 Potsdam Road
Unit 61
Downsview
Ontario M3N 1N3
Canada
Tel: (+1) 416 663 7142
Quarterly newsletter of support, information, sharing and hope for expectant parents experiencing miscarriage.

SIDS Alliance (formerly National Sudden Infant Death Syndrome Foundation)

First Candle/SIDS Alliance
1314 Bedford Avenue
Suite 210
Baltimore
MD 21208
USA
Tel: (in USA) 1 800 221 7437
Website: www.sidsalliance.org

Email: info@firstcandle.org
Promotes infant health and survival in the prenatal period and up to two years of age through programmes of advocacy, education and research. SIDS and other infant death bereavement services are a critical component of its mission.

SPALS (Subsequent Pregnancy After a Loss Support)

Website: www.spals.com
Email:
subscriptions@spals.com (or) michael@spals.com (or) sbgrimes-@juno.com
Support network of about 400 members who have experienced the loss of a child due to miscarriage, selective termination, stillbirth, neonatal death, sudden infant death or accidental death.

Still Fathers

Website: www.stillfathers.org
For fathers who have recently lost a child to SIDS, other infant death or stillbirth.

Unite

c/o Jeanes Hospital
7600 Central Avenue
Philadelphia
PA 19111-2499
USA
Tel: (+1) 215 728 3777 (Tape)
Website: www.unite.freeservers.com
Email: UNITEINC1975@aol.com
Provides grief support services to families after losing a baby due to stillbirth, miscarriage, ectopic pregnancy and early infant death.

Further Reading

Bernstein, Judith. *When the Bough Breaks.* Kansas City: Andrews McMeel Publishing, 1998.

Borg, Susan and Judith Lasker. *When Pregnancy Fails: Families Coping With Miscarriage, Stillbirth, and Infant Death.* Boston: Beacon Press, 1981.

Bramblett, John. *When Good-Bye Is Forever: Learning to Live Again after the Loss of a Child.* New York: Ballantine Books, 1991.

Caplan, Sandi and Gordon Lang. *Grief's Courageous Journey.* Oakland: New Harbinger Publications, 1995.

Coloroso, Barbara. *Parenting Through Crisis: Helping Kids in Times of Loss, Grief and Change.* London: HarperCollins, 2000.

Conrad, Bonnie. *When a Child has Died.* California: Fithian Press, 1995.

Davies, Phyllis. *Grief: Climb Towards Understanding.* California: Sunnybank Publishers, 1996.

Davis, Deborah. *Empty Cradle, Broken Heart: Surviving the Death of Your Baby.* Golden: Fulcrum Publishing, 1991.

Diamond, Kathleen. *Motherhood after Miscarriage.* Avon, Massachusetts: Bob Adams Publishers, 1993.

Donnelly, Katherine. *Recovering from the Loss of a Sibling.* New York: Berkley Publishing Group, 1994.

Douglas, Ann and John Sussman. *Trying Again: A Guide to Pregnancy after Miscarriage, Stillbirth and Infant Loss.* Dallas: Taylor Trade Publishing, 2000.

Farrant, Ann. *Sibling Bereavement: Helping Children Cope with Loss.* New York: Cassell, 1998.

Feeley, Nancy and Laurie Gottlieb. 'Parents' Coping and Communication Following their Infant's Death'. *Omega: Journal of Death and Dying*, Volume 19, Number 1, 1988–9, pp. 51–67.

Finkbeiner, Ann. *After the Death of a Child: Living with Loss through the Years.* Baltimore: Johns Hopkins University Press, 1998.

Fox, Sandy. *I Have No Intention of Saying Goodbye.* Nebraska: Writers' Club Press, 2001.

Gambill, Andrea. *Food for the Soul: A 'Best Of' Bereavement

Poetry Collection. Colorado Springs: Bereavement Publishing, 1996.

Golden, Thomas and James Miller. *When a Man Faces Grief.* Indiana: Willowgreen Publishing, 1998.

Grollman, Rabbi Earl. *Living with Loss, Healing with Hope: A Jewish Perspective.* Boston: Beacon Press, 2000.

Hindmarch, Celia. *On the Death of a Child.* Abingdon: Radcliffe Medical Press, 2000.

Hinton, Clara. *Silent Grief: Miscarriage – Child Loss, Finding Your Way through the Darkness.* Green Forest, Arkansas: New Leaf Press, 1998.

Horchler, Joani and Robin Morris. *The SIDS Survival Guide.* Hyattsville: SIDS Educational Services, 1994.

Hurcombe, Linda. *Losing a Child: Explorations in Grief.* London: Sheldon, 2004.

Kon, Andrea. *How to Survive Bereavement.* London: Hodder, 2002.

Kushner, Harold. *When Bad Things Happen to Good People.* New York: Schocken Books, 2001.

Lake, Tony. *Living with Grief.* London: Sheldon, 2000.

Lanham, Carol Cirulli. *Pregnancy after a Loss: A Guide to Pregnancy after a Miscarriage, Stillbirth or Infant Death.* New York: Berkley Publishing Group, 1999.

Leon, Irving. *When a Baby Dies: Psychotherapy for Pregnancy and Newborn Loss.* New Haven: Yale University Press, 1990.

Lerner, Henry. *Miscarriage: Why It Happens and How Best to Reduce Your Risks.* Cambridge: Perseus Publishing, 2003.

Levang, Elizabeth. *When Men Grieve.* Minneapolis: Fairview Press, 1998.

Lothrop, Hannah and Jane Marie Lamb. *Help, Comfort and Hope after Losing Your Baby in Pregnancy or the First Year.* Cambridge, Massachusetts: Da Capo Press, 2004.

Madill, Betty. *One Step at a Time: Mourning a Child.* Edinburgh: Floris Books, 2001.

Martin, Karen. *When a Baby Dies of SIDS: The Parents' Grief and Search for Reason.* Edmonton: Qual Institute Press, 1998.

Mehren, Elizabeth. *After the Darkest Hour the Sun Will Shine Again.* New York: Simon & Schuster, 1997.

Miller, James and Thomas Golden. *A Man You Know Is Grieving.* Indiana: Willowgreen Publishing, 1998.

Miller, Sukie. *Finding Hope when a Child Dies.* London and New York: Simon & Schuster, 1999.

Nolen-Hoeksema, Dr Susan. *Women Who Think Too Much.* London: Piatkus, 2003.

Rando, Therese, ed. *Parental Loss of a Child.* Champaign: Research Press Company, 1986.

Regan, Lesley. *Miscarriage: What Every Woman Needs to Know.* London: Bloomsbury, 1997.

Roper, Janice. *Dancing on the Moon.* Washington, DC: SIDS Educational Services, 2001.

Schaefer, Dan and Christine Lyons. *How Do We Tell the Children?* New York: Newmarket Press, 1993.

Schaefer, Dan and Christine Lyons. *How Do We Tell The Children? A Parents' Guide to Helping Children Understand and Cope When Someone Dies.* New York: Newmarket Press, 1986.

Scher, Jonathan and Carol Dix. *Preventing Miscarriage: The Good News.* New York: Perennial Currents, 1991.

Schiff, Harriet. *The Bereaved Parent.* New York: Souvenir Press, 1999.

Shaw, Eva. *What To Do when a Loved One Dies.* Irvine: Dickens Press, 1994.

Wiersbe, David. *Gone but Not Lost.* Grand Rapids, Michigan: Baker Books, 1992.

Wunnenberg, Kathe. *Grieving the Child I Never Knew.* Grand Rapids, Michigan: Zondervan Publishing House, 2001.

Index

acupuncture 64
anger 23, 24
anniversaries 20–1
aromatherapy 64–6
Atkins diet 82

baby, being with 15, 62;
    planning for another child
    Chapter 9 *passim*; saying
    goodbye to Chapter 2
    passim, 25
birth defects 9
blighted ovum 4
Bliss 44, 45

ceremony 17
Christmas 20–1
chromosome problems 5
coffee 82
communication 52–4
complementary therapies
    Chapter 8 *passim*
cot death 12–14, 83
counselling 25–6, 55;
    bereavement counselling 31
couple, coping as Chapter 6
    passim

depression 23
diabetes 10
diet *see* nutrition

early baby loss *see* miscarriage
ectopic pregnancy 7
emotional freedom technique
    66–7

environmental stress 4
exercise 23
explanations, searching for
    answers 2

family support Chapter 4
    passim
fathers, implicated in
    miscarriage 4, Chapter 5
    passim
feelings 24–6; *and see* grief
fertility 80
fibroids 81–2
friends Chapter 4 *passim*
funeral arrangements 16–17

genetic counselling 5, 81
genetic problems 3
grief 22, 23–6; in men and
    women 50–2

help and support 34–5, 55;
    from your doctor 31, 86–7
herbalism 67
high blood pressure 10
homeopathy 68–9
hormonal problems 3–4
hypoplasia 33

immune system problems 4
incompetent cervix 4
insensitive comments 27–9

Jeune syndrome 30, 56

massage 82
mementoes 19, 34
memorials 18–20, 56
'milestones' 88–90
miscarriage 1–7, 18;
    age-related risk 1; causes
    3–5; early 2–4; follow–up
    after 5; later 4–5; recurrent
    1; recovery from 6–7
Miscarriage Association 20, 25,
    31
molar pregnancy 7–8
mothering 22

neuro-linguistic programming
    (NLP) 69
nutrition 22, 83–6

other children see siblings
outside world, coping with
    Chapter 4 passim

passive smoking 81
physical care 22–3
placental problems 10
pre-conception care 78–9, 81–6
pre-eclampsia 10, 42
pregnancy: planning Chapter 9
    passim; physical effects of
    22

pregnancy hormones 7, 23
pregnant friends 33

reflexology 70–1
registration of death 16
Reiki 71–2
repeated loss 79–80

SANDS (Stillbirth and
    Neonatal Death Society) 8,
    16, 31, 35
siblings 18; Chapter 7 passim
SIDS see cot death
smoking 83
Still Fathers 39
stillbirth 8–12

traditional Chinese medicine
    (TCM) 72–3

umbilical cord problems 10
uterus, structural problems 4–5

work, return to 33–4
World Health Organization
    (WHO) 9
worry, controlling 90–2

yoga 73–4